THE
ROTH IRA
Made Simple

Gary R. Trock, E.A.

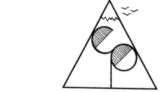

Conquest Publishing, Inc.
Griffith, Indiana

The information in this book is intended to provide general guidelines on matters of interest to individual taxpayers. The application and impact of tax laws can vary widely from case to case, however, based upon the specific or unique facts involved. Accordingly, this book is not intended to serve as legal, accounting, or tax advice. Since tax laws and regulations change frequently, readers are encouraged to seek competent professional advice for their individual situation. The author and publisher cannot be held responsible for positions taken or losses incurred as a result of the application of any information contained in this book.

Conquest Publishing, Inc.
P.O. Box 543
Griffith, Indiana 46319

Email: conquestpublishing@yahoo.com

ISBN: 0-9666227-0-7

Library of Congress Catalog Card Number: 98-96454

*To my wife, Georgene, and my
daughters, Kristy, Stacey, and Lindsey,
who tolerated me during this process.*

About the author...

As an enrolled agent and practicing tax professional, Gary R. Trock has more than 20 years of extensive accounting and tax experience. Since successfully started his own bookkeeping, accounting, and tax practice in 1980, Trock has developed a keen insight for getting his clients the best tax breaks and benefits. He has represented individuals and small business corporations in numerous IRS audits and appeals proceedings. In addition, he offers business, tax, and financial planning services.

Since the creation of the Roth IRA in 1997, Trock has helped clients determine the advantages and disadvantages of choosing a Roth IRA. He quickly realized that converting a traditional IRA to a Roth IRA is not automatically the best choice for everyone. Every situation requires a careful analysis of several major factors. To help identify these factors, Trock wrote *The Roth IRA Made Simple.* In it he also explains elements of the Roth that are not widely understood and that may impact a decision on contributing or converting to a Roth IRA. His book is an extremely helpful tool, in layman's language, for those needing guidance with Roth IRA planning.

Introduction

The new Roth IRA is a boon for most taxpayers—but not all.

The Roth IRA Made Simple explains the basics and benefits of this new retirement account option. The book points out useful strategies for maximizing your Roth IRA and details factors you will need to consider before you decide to contribute or convert to a Roth IRA.

Many comparisons of the traditional and Roth IRAs show you areas of concern for your particular tax situation. They demonstrate why early action on a Roth IRA *may* mean a financial boost for you.

Easy-to-follow examples help you understand qualifications for traditional and Roth IRAs, the differences in the two types of accounts, and ways you can assist your children or grandchildren through the new Roth alternative.

The book clarifies the Roth IRA so you can determine whether this remarkable retirement opportunity is for you.

Contents

CHAPTER 1

What Is a Roth IRA?

If you haven't heard about the Roth IRA (Individual Retirement Account) by now, you will! If you have heard about it, you're probably in a quandary. The word is out, and just about every financial institution is touting it. You're hearing about it on radio, TV, the Internet, newspapers, and magazines. The coverage is unrelenting and creating quite an interest in this new retirement savings bonanza. So now the question is, what is a Roth IRA and why did our government create such a wonderful savings vehicle?

Reason for This New Retirement Sensation

The following explains it in a nutshell. It is from the congressional committee report having to do with the creation of the Roth IRA through the Taxpayer Relief Act of 1997:

The committee believes that some individuals would be more likely to save if funds set aside in a tax-favored account could be withdrawn without tax after a reasonable holding period for retirement or certain special purposes. Some taxpayers may find such a vehicle more suitable for their savings needs.

Based on that statement, it sounds like there really is someone in Congress listening to the needs of the American taxpayer!

In order to define the Roth IRA better, let me begin by briefing you about the "traditional" IRA. Prior to the Taxpayer Relief Act of 1997, traditional IRAs were the only vehicles for many individuals wanting to save for retirement while deferring taxes. Congress originally created these IRAs in the 1970s.

Our government felt at the time that many individuals were not covered by retirement plans of their employers and much more was needed to assist them financially. The concern was that our Social Security system was not going to be financially sufficient to cover the required benefits into the future (which, unfortunately, still appears true today).

That kind of concern brought about several changes to IRAs. More specifically, Congress has expanded and liberalized IRAs to include more individuals. A "traditional IRA" is the type you can deduct on your tax return if you qualify, thus enabling individuals to get a tax savings for their contribution. Qualifying generally means that you are not an active participant in an employer-sponsored retirement plan, i.e., a 401(k) plan or profit-sharing plan, or if your employer covers you, your adjusted gross income is below a specified amount. Even if you don't qualify, you are still able to contribute to what is known as the *non-deductible* traditional IRA.

With the traditional IRAs, whether deductible or not, contributions and earnings would accumulate *tax-deferred.* This deferral effectively allows your investments to grow unencumbered by income taxes for a certain period of time, a real advantage for growing your retirement nest egg. Unfortunately, the time will come when you'll have to square up with Uncle Sam. This occurs when you begin to take withdrawals from your account. This isn't really such a bad deal since you probably took the tax deductions in years in which you were in higher tax brackets than you will be during retirement. Let's face it; that's usually the motivating reason for using a traditional deductible IRA. It was and still is a great deduction for millions of taxpayers, that is, until Congress passed the Taxpayer Relief Act of 1997 and gave birth to the Roth IRA, a new non-deductible type of IRA with exciting advantages and possibilities for even more taxpayers.

The Big Advantage

Although the Roth IRA has many of the same characteristics as a non-deductible traditional IRA, one of its most astounding benefits is that distributions (withdrawals) from it will be *tax-free*! In other words, *all the earnings* that will accumulate in the account can never be taxed if certain conditions are met. It sure sounds like this is too good to be true. Hopefully, this option for retirement funds will be with us for a long time.

This stunning advantage sets the Roth IRA apart from the traditional type and has created an unprecedented national interest. According to an April 7, 1998, article in the *Chicago Sun-Times*, major mutual fund companies have said they are opening huge numbers of Roth

3

accounts. The article went on to say that Americans who are looking to increase their retirement savings were spurring tremendous interest in the Roth IRA tax-break—exactly what Congress was hoping for.

From my own perspective, I was truly amazed at how many clients are expressing interest in Roth IRAs. During last tax season, a week didn't go by without a multitude of inquiries from clients about it. The idea of taking money out of a retirement plan tax-free is quite extraordinary in itself. I personally can't recall anything that generated this much interest in my 27 years experience in the accounting and tax profession.

Other Features

In addition to the tax-free benefit, as with the traditional IRA certain early distributions for first-time homebuyers, costs of higher education, and certain medical expenses are not subject to the early withdrawal penalty (see Chapter 6 for detailed information on early withdrawals).

Unlike traditional IRAs, there are no mandatory withdrawals once you have reached age 70½. Besides that, you can continue to fund your Roth IRA beyond age 70½ as long as you have earned income and you stay within certain income guidelines.

Contributions to a Roth IRA

Roth IRA contributions begin for the year 1998. Individuals are permitted to contribute up to $2,000 per year provided that certain conditions are met (see Chapter 2 for further discussion).

Due Date for Establishing a Roth IRA

In order to contribute to a Roth IRA for a particular year, you will need to create the account by April 15 of the following year. This is the same date requirement as for the actual contribution itself. In fact, it's the same due date as for traditional IRAs. You will not be allowed to file for an extension of time to establish the Roth IRA. Keep in mind that if you are going to have to set up the account via the mail, you will need ample time to allow for delivery. Some mutual fund companies will not accept the postmark date as the date of receipt. Avoid these unnecessary obstacles and possible loss of contribution by setting it up early!

Due Date for Contributing to Your Roth IRA

Contributions to Roth IRAs were allowed beginning with the calendar year 1998. As with traditional IRAs, you have until April 15 to make Roth IRA contributions for the preceding calendar year, the same due date as your income tax return. You cannot extend the time by filing an extension. For example, if you wanted to contribute for the year 1998, you would have until April 15, 1999, to do so. Obviously, it would be in your best interest to fund the account as early as you can in order to start the earnings accumulation process.

Maximum Contribution for All IRAs

If you are also considering contributions to a traditional IRA, keep in mind that your aggregate contribution to all IRAs (excluding Education IRAs, SEP IRAs, and SIMPLE IRAs) is limited to a maximum of $2,000 per individual. Let's say, for example, you would like to contribute $1,500 to a traditional IRA to get the tax deduction; then you would be limited to only a $500 contribution to a Roth IRA.

Converting Your Traditional IRA to a Roth IRA

Rolling over IRAs has been a possibility for some time. You may have had many reasons for doing so in the past, one of which was because a new trustee offered a different selection of investments (i.e., individual stocks vs. mutual funds).

Now there is another important reason to do a rollover, and that is moving your funds into a Roth IRA and getting tax-free rather than tax-deferred earnings. Rolling over (converting) is now an option for many taxpayers. Chapter 5 will cover this area in more detail. The due date for completing your *conversion* is the last day of the year in which you choose to convert, not the due date of the tax return for that year. This should not be confused with the due date for a Roth IRA *contribution*.

<u>Summing it Up</u>

In summary, the Roth IRA is a new, after-tax, non-deductible IRA featuring tax-deferred earnings, tax-free distributions, and more liberal contribution and distribution options. Annual contributions of up to $2,000 per individual are allowed, subject to certain conditions (see Chapter 2).

Thanks to Senator William Roth and the passage of the Taxpayer Relief Act of 1997, the Roth IRA will soon become one of the most attractive savings, financial, and retirement planning vehicles of all times.

CHAPTER 2

Who Qualifies for a Roth IRA and How Much Can I Contribute?

Meeting Two Conditions

Beginning with the calendar year 1998, individuals can make contributions up to $2,000 to a Roth IRA under two specific conditions. The *first condition* is that you must have **earned income.** Earned income includes wages, salaries, professional fees, tips, bonuses, and commissions. Earned income can be found on your W-2 (box 1) and Schedule C (earnings from self-employment). Earned income is generally income that is derived from providing personal services, with the exception of alimony and separate maintenance. Alimony and separate maintenance, while not considered earned income, is treated as compensation and will count towards meeting the earned income condition. Interest income, dividends, capital gains, pension or annuity income, rental income from real estate, or Social Security benefits are not considered earned income and do not count towards it.

The *second condition* you will have to meet in order to qualify for a Roth IRA contribution is for your "modified" adjusted gross income (MAGI) not to exceed certain limits. Different filing statuses have different MAGI limits. This frightening-looking description can turn you off rather quickly. To combat that urge and to keep things simple, we will be referring to adjusted gross income (AGI) from here on. Modified adjusted gross income, I might add, does not apply to many taxpayers since it has to do with making adjustments to income for items such as employer-provided adoption expenses, interest on U.S. Savings Bonds used to pay higher education expenses, and foreign earned income that was excluded from taxable income.

You must know also that a deduction for a traditional IRA will not count towards your AGI limit. In other words, the deduction is to be added back to income in determining if you've exceeded the AGI limit for a Roth IRA contribution for your filing status. This was one of the corrections under the Internal Revenue Service Restructuring and Reform Act of 1998.

Single Filers

If you are filing your income tax return as "single" or "head of household" and want to contribute the maximum $2,000 to your Roth IRA, you will need to show that you have at least $2,000 in earned income. If earned income is less than $2,000, then that lesser amount will be your maximum allowable contribution.

Single and head of household taxpayers will need to have an AGI of no more than $95,000 to contribute the maximum of $2,000. If your AGI is over $95,000, a

phase-out of the contribution begins. It will be
completely phased out when your AGI reaches $110,000
(see Figure 2-2). If you fall somewhere in between the
phase-out range limits, your allowable contribution will
be determined by dividing the excess of your AGI over
$95,000 by $15,000. The resulting percentage will be the
portion of $2,000 that is disallowed. For example, let's
say your AGI is $98,000. Your allowable Roth IRA
contribution would be $1,600 as shown below:

$98,000-95,000 = $3,000 (excess over $95,000)

$3,000/15,000 = .20 or 20% (amount disallowed)

20% of $2,000 = $400 (amount disallowed)

$2,000-400 = **$1,600** (maximum allowed)

To aid you in determining if you qualify for a Roth
IRA, please refer to the flow chart in Figure 2-3.

> ### *Be Aware:*
> Even teenage children are allowed a
> Roth IRA contribution as long as they
> have earned income--a very rewarding
> planning opportunity! Imagine the
> growth in this account! See Figure 2-1.

Value of Roth IRA (Starting Age:15)
Annual contribution: $2,000

At Age	Rates of return			
	6%	8%	10%	12%
25	27,943	31,291	35,062	39,309
45	167,603	244,692	361,887	540,585
65	615,512	1,239,344	2,560,599	5,376,041

Fig. 2-1

Married Filers

If you are married and filing jointly and want to contribute the maximum of $2,000 each ($4,000 total), all you need to show is at least $4,000 of earned income was made by *either* spouse. It does not matter that there is a non-working spouse; you will still be able to contribute $2,000 to each of the Roth IRA accounts. If your combined earned income is less than $4,000, then that lesser amount will be your maximum allowable contribution, divided (any way you wish or equally) between accounts.

Be aware:
Individuals who are married but file their tax returns as "married filing separately" are allowed a limited Roth IRA contribution. The exception to this occurs if the couple lives apart at all times during the year. In this case, the separately filing couple can qualify for a Roth IRA contribution as if they each were single.

Married taxpayers filing jointly must have an AGI of no more than $150,000 to qualify for the maximum Roth IRA contribution of $2,000 each or $4,000 total. If your combined AGI exceeds $150,000, the phase-out begins and the contribution is completely gone when $160,000 is reached (see Figure 2-2). When your combined AGI falls between $150,000 and $160,000, your maximum allowable contribution is reduced. It will be determined by dividing the excess of your AGI over $150,000 by $10,000. The resulting percentage will be the portion of $2,000 that is disallowed for each spouse. Let's say your AGI is $158,000. Your allowable Roth IRA contribution would be $400 each or $800 total, as shown below.

$158,000-150,000= $8,000 (excess over $150,000)

$8,000/10,000 = .80 or 80% (amount disallowed)
80% of $2,000 = $1,600 each

$1,600 X 2 =$3,200 (disallowed contribution for both)

$4,000-$3,200 = **$800** (maximum allowed for both)

To aid you in determining if you qualify for a Roth IRA, please refer to the flow chart in Figure 2-4.

Be aware:
When determining a contribution to a Roth IRA, it makes no difference that you are an active participant in an employer-sponsored retirement plan.

Roth IRA Contribution Phase-Out Range

Phase-out starts when AGI is over:	Phase-out is completed when AGI reaches:
Single and Head of Household filers:	
$95,000	**$110,000**
Married Couples:	
$150,000	**$160,000**
Married Filing Separately:	
-0-	**$10,000**

Fig. 2-2

Be aware:

Excess contributions to your Roth IRA will be subject to a 6% tax, so be sure your allowable contribution is correct.

An excerpt from an explanation of the Roth IRA prepared by the staff of the Senate Finance Committee adds:

These complex income limits were not part of Senator Roth's initial proposal for the Roth IRA, as passed by the Senate. However, these limits were imposed by the Clinton Administration as a part of Administration's support for the Taxpayer Relief Act.

Qualifying for the Roth IRA Contribution

Filing Status: Single or Head of Household

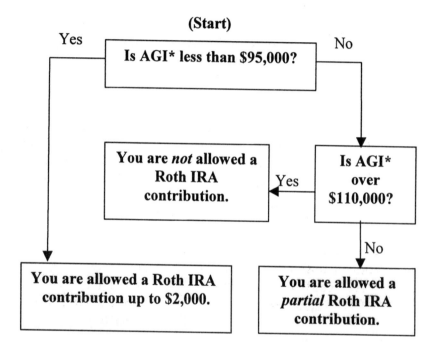

* Adjusted gross income
(Assumption: Earned income of individual is at least $2,000)

Fig. 2-3

<u>Qualifying for the Roth IRA Contribution</u>

Filing Status: Married Filing Jointly

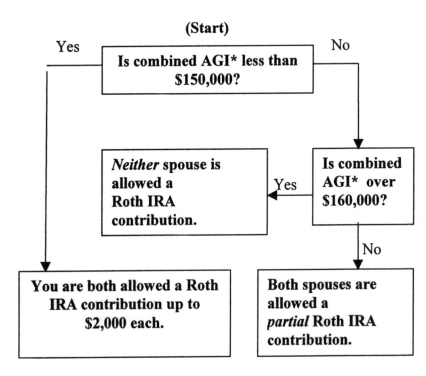

*Adjusted gross income
(Assumption: Earned income of each individual is at least $2,000 or
$4,000 for one spouse)

<u>Fig. 2-4</u>

Qualifying for the Roth IRA Contribution

Filing Status: Married Filing Separately

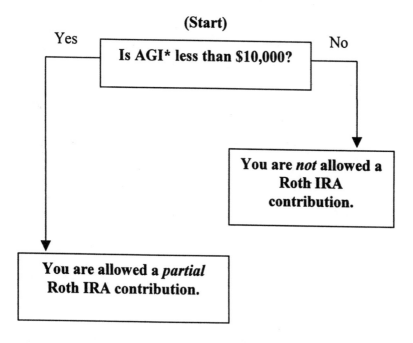

(Start)

Yes **Is AGI* less than $10,000?** No

You are *not* allowed a Roth IRA contribution.

You are allowed a *partial* Roth IRA contribution.

* Adjusted gross income
(Assumption: Earned income of individual is at least $2,000)

Fig. 2-5

Strategies to Consider

On Reducing Adjusted Gross Income (AGI)

As previously mentioned, you have to *qualify* for a Roth IRA contribution. This means that your adjusted gross income (AGI) must be below a certain amount and you must have earned income (as discussed earlier in this chapter).

There are many different moves you can make to become a candidate for a Roth IRA. The following ideas serve as a guide to helping you get your AGI below the threshold amounts for making contributions or conversions to Roth IRAs. These can be extremely important if you're on the borderline in qualifying for your Roth IRA.

1. Consider reallocating taxable dividend- and interest-paying stocks and bonds to tax-free municipal bonds or municipal bond funds. You may even consider investments in growth stocks (very little, if any, taxable dividends are paid).

2. Try moving taxable interest-bearing accounts (savings accounts, money market accounts) to U.S. Savings Bonds. This allows you to defer the taxation of the interest until later years. This should be done only when you know the funds are not needed in the near term (12+ years).

3.   Try to put off the sale of any capital asset that will produce a gain in the current year. If this gain is a one-time gain and is sizable, make sure you can time it so that it won't hurt you in the year you defer it to. This strategy is especially helpful in a year in which you do a conversion from a traditional IRA to a Roth IRA.

4.   When possible, try having year-end bonuses paid in the subsequent year. This strategy has to be handled with a little more planning. If your bonus is considered earned and "constructively received" in the current year, even though the actual payment is in the following year, the delayed payment may not benefit you. The pay date arrangement with your employer must be done prior to the "earning" of the bonus.

Tax regulations describe constructive receipt of income as such: "*Income although not actually reduced to a taxpayer's possession is constructively received by him in the taxable year during which it is credited to his account, set apart for him, or otherwise made available so that he may draw upon it at any time, or so that he could have drawn upon it during the taxable year if notice of intention to withdraw had been given. However, income is not constructively received if the taxpayer's control of its receipt is subject to substantial limitations or restrictions.*"

5.   If you are considering dumping a losing stock, try selling it before year-end. Be aware that the maximum capital loss in any year is limited to

$3,000. Also note that you can net capital gains with capital losses. In other words, you might already have realized a capital gain of, say, $10,000 on the sale of another stock and would like to sell your losing stock and incur a loss of $13,000. In this case, you can net the gain and loss to end up with a net capital loss of $3,000. Here you have effectively reduced your AGI by $13,000. If your loss were any larger, it would have to be carried forward to following years until used up.

This capital loss strategy may work with other capital assets as well. Another example would be the personal loan to that "ex" friend you cannot or will not be able to collect. In this case, the bad loan would probably qualify for a non-business bad debt. This loss is treated as a short-term capital loss for tax purposes, subject to the maximum of $3,000 per year.

Selling that silver bullion or silver coins you bought in the 1980s may be another possible capital loss you might consider (unfortunately).

6. If you own a business (C corporation), try taking a lesser salary. If your corporation has a note payable to you on the books, consider taking principal and interest as opposed to salary. The principal amounts will not be treated as income to you.

7. If you are in business as a sole proprietor, consider setting up a Keogh Plan, Simplified Employee

Pension (SEP), or Savings Incentive Match Plan for Employees (SIMPLE). These are retirement plans that, if set up in time, can significantly reduce your current taxable income and AGI. The Keogh Plan must be set up before your business tax year ends but can be funded up until you file your income tax return (including extensions). The SEP can be set up **and** funded by the filing due date of your tax return (including extensions). The SIMPLE plan will also have to be set up before year-end, but you will have different funding requirements. By the way, under the tax law changes in 1998, it is now clear that you can contribute to a Roth IRA (assuming you qualify) even though you contribute to either a SEP or SIMPLE in the same year.

8.   If you have income derived from a sole proprietorship, partnership, or S Corporation, try delaying billing and/or collections (depending on method of accounting--cash or accrual basis). If you use the cash basis method of accounting, try deferring collections to the next year and accelerating expenses into the current year. If you use the accrual method of accounting, try deferring end-of-year billing and "incur" expenses that are ordinary and necessary for the current year.

9.   If you are an owner in a pass-through entity (S corporation, partnership, and certain LLCs) or sole proprietorship business that hasn't purchased any significant amount of furniture, fixtures, or equipment in the current year, consider doing so

by year-end. Under Section 179 of the IRS Code, you can elect to expense rather than to depreciate these assets. The assets must be purchased **and** placed in service by your year-end. The maximum amount you can expense is $19,000 for 1999. This limit works its way up to $25,000 by the year 2003. This can be a great way to bring down your taxable income.

10. If you're an owner in a pass-through entity or sole proprietorship (using cash-basis accounting), consider prepaying up to one year of business insurance premiums.

11. If you are an owner of real estate rental property, you can accelerate expenses into the current year. That repair work you were contemplating doing next year should be done this year. Be careful not to exceed your maximum passive activity loss allowed.

12. If you plan on selling a piece of real estate (not your principal residence) or business property and you know there will be a sizable taxable gain, consider a like-kind exchange. This will allow your gain to be deferred until a later date. This type of transaction is often referred to as a Section 1031 exchange (referencing the IRS Code section). Time and additional planning are required with these types of moves, but the payoff can reward the effort.

13. If you are involved in an elective salary deferral plan like a 401(k), consider maximizing your tax-deferred contribution amount, especially if your

employer is matching portions of your contribution.

Paying College Costs

If you plan on helping to pay for college costs for your grandchildren in the next five or more years and are at least age 59½ by then, consider making contributions to a Roth IRA early. You'll be able to withdraw funds both tax-free and penalty-free. Just be sure that you do not withdraw the funds before the five-tax-year holding period has passed. The five-tax-year holding period starts when the *very first* Roth IRA contribution is made. It does not matter that you have several Roth IRA accounts or when each of them was started. The 1998 act made clear that you did not have to keep contributory and conversion Roth IRA accounts separate anymore. All your Roth IRA accounts will now be treated as if they were one account. This was a big relief and saved taxpayers from a lot of record keeping.

Be aware:
Since the IRS now treats all Roth IRA accounts as one, making an early token ($100) Roth IRA contribution will start the five-tax-year waiting period clock for all Roth IRAs.

As an example of the foregoing, let's say Grandpa and Grandma (both age 55) have a granddaughter, Lisa, who will be attending college in five years. By having Grandpa and Grandma each contribute (assuming they qualify) $2,000 annually to a Roth IRA for the next five years, they will be able to withdraw all or any portion of their Roth IRA account, tax-free and penalty-free, to cover college costs for Lisa. The Roth IRA accounts will be approximately $23,900 (assuming 8% return) in value after five years. That's $3,900 earned with no tax! Even an Education IRA for Lisa cannot beat that in five years. Besides that, this strategy fits well for those doing some estate planning. Grandpa and Grandma are each allowed to gift up to $10,000 to Lisa for a total of $20,000 in one year.

Children's Roth IRAs

1.   If you have a teenage child working part-time and earning at least $2,000 during the year, he or she qualifies for the maximum contribution to a Roth IRA. Let's assume that your child prefers to spend this income on personal items rather than contributing to a Roth IRA. If the parents want to save for the child's future, they now have the incentive to do so. The thing to do now is sock away as much as possible (up to the $2,000 limit) into the child's Roth IRA. By contributing to your child's Roth account, you are effectively "gifting" money to him or her—perfectly legally. This move can also pave the way for that child to have enough money in the Roth IRA account to make a tax-free and penalty-free withdrawal for a first-time home purchase (up to $10,000).

Grandparents can also gift to your child's Roth IRA account if so desired.

2. If you are self-employed and would like to employ your child in the business, you may be pleasantly surprised to realize the tax benefits you stand to gain. By hiring your child, you'll not only get the deduction for his or her wages, but you'll create the earned income needed to fund a Roth IRA for him or her.

Another great benefit from this move is that the child may not even be subject to income tax on the wages. Assuming your child has no other taxable income, he or she can earn up to $4,300 (1999 standard deduction) and pay no income tax. Keep in mind that your child must actually work for you, the pay must be reasonable, and you'll need to file the respective tax forms, including W-2s for the year.

If the dependent child is also under the age of 18, he or she is exempt from any Social Security tax.

The following example will illustrate the effects of this move:

In 1999, daughter Sally, age 16, earns $4,000 working for her father in his sole proprietorship. The parents have net earnings from the business of $65,000 (their only income) before Sally's wages.

Amount of tax parents save:

Income tax saved = $806

Social Security tax saved = $565

Total taxes saved: $1,371

Interesting note: The amount of taxes saved is close to the amount needed to fund Sally's Roth IRA! Outside of perhaps a small amount of state income tax, this appears to be a win-win situation. Isn't it nice to know that the government may be paying for most of the investment in Sally's Roth IRA?

3. If you have the financial resources, you can take item 2 above even further. Consider setting up a SIMPLE plan (Savings Incentive Match Plan for Employees).

    Let's assume Sally, age 18, works for her father in the sole proprietorship in 1999 and earns $10,000 (her only income). The parents have net earnings from the business of $65,000 (their only income) before Sally's wages. Sally wants to participate in the SIMPLE plan, have the maximum ($6,000) withheld from her pay during the year, and would like to contribute to a Roth IRA for 1999 (her parents must be proud of her). Here is how this will fare:

Amount of tax parents save:

Income tax = $1,642
Social Security tax = 1,413
State income tax (4% est.) = 400

Total tax saved = $3,455

Tax effect on Sally:

Total income ...$10,000
Less: SIMPLE plan deduction...... 6,000
Sub-total   4,000
Less: Standard deduction............... 4,300
Taxable income   None

Federal income tax.............................-0-
Social Security tax $1,530
State income tax (4% est.)   160
Total tax............................. $1,690

Sally is not exempt from Social Security tax, however, since she is age 18 or older. But the benefits are that she was able to put away $8,300 into tax-deferred and tax-free investments ($6,000 SIMPLE, $2,000 Roth IRA, and her father should be making a matching contribution up to 3% of Sally's wages, or $300, into her SIMPLE plan).

In effect the family as a whole has benefited by saving $1,765 ($3,455-$1,690) in taxes and was able to get Sally a good head start on her future.

If Sally were to quit her job after two years (two-year rule) from the day her father made her first contribution into Sally's SIMPLE plan, Sally would be allowed a qualified rollover contribution into a Roth IRA account. As you can imagine, this can be an excellent way of getting Sally a jump-start on her Roth IRA.

Problems to Ponder

Marriage Problems

1.   If you're thinking of getting married in the current year and you contributed to a Roth IRA (or anticipated doing so), be careful. When your income and that of your would-be spouse are combined, be sure they do not exceed the applicable dollar amounts for AGI for married persons (Figure 2-2). If the AGI is over the limits, you will lose your qualification to have a Roth IRA for the year. If you have contributed to it and later find out that you don't qualify, you will be able to transfer it to a traditional IRA (if you qualify) by the deadline for filing your income tax for that year.

2.   If your marriage is dissolved by December 31 of the current year, you may also have a problem if you thought of investing in a Roth IRA for the year. The problem lies with your filing status as of the last day of the year. For example, let's suppose John and Mary (no children) became divorced before the year was out. Tax law says that they will be filing as single rather than as married filing jointly. John's income is $115,000, and he is covered by his employer's plan. Mary's income is $35,000, and she also is covered by her employer's plan. They both thought of having a

Roth IRA for the year. After the divorce, only Mary can have one. John lost his possibility because he has exceeded the phase-out range for a single person's AGI ($110,000). Mary did not. Mary can also split her IRA contribution into both types of IRAs if she desires.

Regarding IRS Audits

If your 1040 is chosen for audit in a year in which you contributed to a Roth IRA (or deductible IRA for this purpose), and they made upward adjustments to your income, you could possibly lose the contribution. This can happen if the change to your AGI is significant enough that you will have exceeded your phase-out range. Be sure that items of income and deduction can stand up to the scrutiny of the IRS.

CHAPTER 3

Understanding the
Traditional IRA
(The Deductible Type)

A discussion of the traditional *deductible* IRA is necessary in a book about Roth IRAs because deciding which IRA is best for an individual is an important question. Should you contribute to a traditional IRA or a Roth IRA is one of the most common questions initially. In light of the Roth IRA (a non-deductible type itself), it doesn't make a lot of sense for anyone (who qualifies) to be interested in the traditional *non-deductible* IRA. This is primarily true because that vehicle merely offers a *tax-deferred* rather than a *tax-free* accumulation of earnings. Sure, there can be a situation where the traditional non-deductible IRA might be used (i.e., taxpayers who don't qualify because AGI exceeds the limit), but in my opinion, if you qualify, there are very few circumstances in which a Roth IRA contribution won't be to your advantage. Having said that, little will be mentioned in this book regarding the use of the traditional *non-deductible* IRA.

Prior to enactment of the Taxpayer Relief Act of 1997, individuals had the opportunity, subject to certain conditions, of choosing between a deductible IRA and the non-deductible IRA. This still holds true today except that there's the added choice of the Roth IRA.

There have also been some very interesting enhancements to traditional IRAs. One of the most appealing has been the increase in the adjusted gross income limit used for a spouse not participating in an employer-sponsored retirement plan. The limit was raised from $50,000 to $150,000.

Qualifying for Traditional Deductible IRAs

Single filers who are *not* active participants in an employer-sponsored retirement plan

In order to qualify for a traditional deductible IRA, an individual needs to have earned income. If you are seeking the maximum deduction amount of $2,000, your earned income will have to be at least $2,000. If your earned income is under that amount, your deduction will be limited to that lesser amount.

There is no limitation as to what your adjusted gross income can be. The idea behind this is apparent. The government is allowing those without any retirement plan the incentive to start their own without any hitches.

Single filers who *are* active participants in an employer-sponsored retirement plan

Again an individual wanting a traditional deductible IRA needs to have earned income. To maximize the deductible amount of $2,000, you need at least $2,000 in earned income. Any earned income below this amount is the limit for the deduction. In addition to that, your adjusted gross income (AGI) cannot exceed $30,000 for 1998 to maximize the deduction. Figure 3-1 defines the applicable dollar amounts for phasing out your deduction in later years. The government in its infinite wisdom has already come up with the phase-out dollar amounts for future years.

Notice how the annual increase is $1,000 a year, but in year 2003 it jumps $6,000. Why then does it rise by only $5,000 in the year 2004? Unless Congress has a crystal ball on future inflation indexing, you have to wonder how they arrived at such numbers.

Phase-out Ranges for Use in Determining Deductible Traditional IRA Contributions For:		
Single and Head of Household Filers (With active participation in employer retirement plan)		
	Phase-out begins when AGI is: (lower limit)	Phase-out is completed when AGI reaches: (upper limit)
Year 1998	30,000	40,000
Year 1999	31,000	41,000
Year 2000	32,000	42,000
Year 2001	33,000	43,000
Year 2002	34,000	44,000
Year 2003	40,000	50,000
Year 2004	45,000	55,000
After 2004	50,000	60,000

Fig. 3-1

If your AGI exceeds the upper dollar limit, no deductible IRA is allowed.

Example 1: You have earned income of $25,000, and your AGI is $29,000 (without an IRA deduction) for the year 1998. Your maximum deductible contribution would be $2,000.

Reason: You were below the lower dollar limitation of AGI, even though you were covered by an employer-sponsored retirement plan.

Example 2: You have earned income of $25,000, and your AGI is $42,000 (without an IRA deduction) for the year 1998. You are *not* allowed a deductible contribution for 1998.

Reason: You've exceeded the upper dollar limitation of AGI ($40,000) (see Figure 3-1) *and* you were covered by an employer-sponsored retirement plan.

Be aware:
If you did not qualify for a deductible IRA, a Roth IRA may still be an alternative. See Chapter 2 for its qualifications.

If your adjusted gross income were within the applicable range for a given year, as shown in Figure 3-1, you would begin to see your deduction whittled down, if not completely lost. To help you determine a deductible contribution when you're in this situation, we'll use the phase-out range for the year 1998. The deductible amount will be determined by taking the excess over $30,000 and dividing it by $10,000. The $10,000 amount is a constant number; it is the difference between the upper and lower dollar limits. The resulting percentage will be the portion of the $2,000 that is disallowed. Let's say, for example, that you have an AGI (including enough earned income) of $34,000. This would allow for a deductible contribution of only $1,200 as shown below:

$34,000-30,000 = $4,000 (excess over $30,000)

$4,000/10,000 = .40 or 40% (amount disallowed)

40% of $2,000 = $800 (disallowed)

$2,000-800 = **$1,200** (maximum contribution allowed)

To aid you in determining if you qualify for a deductible IRA, please refer to the flow chart in Figure 3-3.

Be aware:
The AGI phase-out ranges (Figure 3-1) do not take into account the traditional IRA *deduction* itself. This means you cannot count the IRA deduction in arriving at AGI.

Married filers of whom one or both are employed and *neither* is active in an employer-sponsored retirement plan

In this situation, both spouses are permitted to contribute to traditional deductible IRAs. To max out your contribution of $4,000 ($2,000 for each account), you would need to show that *either* spouse has earned income of at least $4,000. Any amount below this would be the maximum allowable contribution and deduction.

Here too there is no limitation as to how high your adjusted gross income can be. The intent is to allow those without retirement plans the opportunity to create their own.

Married filers who *are both* active participants in employer-sponsored retirement plans

In order for both spouses to contribute the maximum to traditional deductible IRAs, or $2,000 each, there needs to be earned income of at least $4,000 between both of you. It doesn't matter that one spouse has less than $2,000 in earned income. In addition to that, combined adjusted gross income (AGI) should not exceed $50,000 (lower limit) for 1998. If combined AGI exceeds $50,000, a phase-out of the deduction begins. The deduction is completely phased out when combined AGI reaches $60,000 (upper limit). Figure 3-2 defines the applicable dollar amounts for the phasing out of your deduction in later years.

Married filers of which only *one* spouse is covered by an employer-sponsored retirement plan

In an effort by Congress to expand the benefits for those without any retirement plan, the new law allows for deductible IRA contributions for spouses not active in an employer-sponsored retirement plan.

As long as either spouse has earned income of at least $4,000 and the couple's combined adjusted gross income (AGI) is below $150,000, the spouse not covered by a retirement plan is permitted to contribute to a deductible IRA. The contribution can be for the maximum amount of $2,000. The spouse that *is* covered by the employer plan is not allowed a deductible IRA contribution if their AGI is over $60,000 (1998).

If your combined adjusted gross income exceeds $160,000, no deduction is allowed for either spouse. This range of $150,000 to $160,000 happens to be another dollar amount limitation or phase-out range under the new law.

Combined adjusted gross income between $150,000 and $160,000 would allow for a partial deductible contribution for the spouse without a plan. The deduction will be determined by dividing the excess of AGI over $150,000 by $10,000. The resulting percentage will be the portion of the $2,000 that is disallowed. For example, if the combined AGI were $156,000 (including enough earned income), the maximum deductible contribution would be $800 for the spouse without a retirement plan, as shown below:

$156,000-150,000 = $6,000 (excess over $150,000)

$6,000/10,000 = .60 or 60% (amount disallowed)

60% of $2,000 = $1,200 (disallowed)

$2,000-1,200 = **$800** (deductible contribution)

To aid you in determining if you qualify for a deductible IRA, please refer to the flow chart in Figure 3-4.

Phase-Out Ranges for Use in Determining Traditional Deductible IRA Contributions For:		
<u>Married filers</u> (with active participation in employer retirement plan)		
	Phase-out begins when AGI is: (lower limit)	Phase-out completed when AGI reaches: (upper limit)
Year 1998	50,000	60,000
Year 1999	51,000	61,000
Year 2000	52,000	62,000
Year 2001	53,000	63,000
Year 2002	54,000	64,000
Year 2003	60,000	70,000
Year 2004	65,000	75,000
Year 2005	70,000	80,000
Year 2006	75,000	85,000
After 2006	80,000	90,000

<u>Fig. 3-2</u>

These phase-out ranges are used for each individual spouse with active participation in an employer-sponsored retirement plan.

Be aware:
You cannot count the IRA deduction in determining AGI for Figure 3-2

Example 1: Husband has earned income of $60,000, wife has earned income of $90,000; and other income totals $10,000 for a combined AGI of $160,000 for 1999. *Neither* spouse is active in any employer retirement plan. Both individuals can choose a traditional deductible IRA of up to $2,000 each.

Reason: Since neither spouse is covered by an employer retirement plan, there is no limit as to how much their AGI can be.

Example 2: Husband has earned income of $45,000; wife has earned income of $3,000; and other income totals $1,000 for a combined AGI of $49,000 for 1999. *Both* are active in an employer retirement plan. Both individuals can choose a traditional deductible IRA of up to $2,000 each.

Reason: Since their combined AGI for 1999 is less than the lower limit ($51,000) of the phase-out range (see Figure 3-2), there is no loss of or phasing out of an IRA deduction.

Example 3: Husband has earned income of $90,000; wife has earned income of $50,000; and other income totals $5,000 for a combined AGI of $145,000 in 1999. The husband is an active participant in an employer retirement plan; the wife is not. Only the wife is permitted to deduct up to $2,000 for a traditional deductible IRA.

Reason: Even though their combined AGI is above the upper limit of the phase-out range of $61,000, it is below the new higher $150,000 limit amount with respect to spouses not active in an employer plan. The wife is allowed the deduction. The husband will be denied the opportunity because he is covered by a plan and their combined AGI exceeds the upper limit of the phase-out range for 1999 (see Figure 3-2).

Example 4: Same facts as example 3 except wife has earned income of $60,000 and AGI is $175,000. The wife is denied a deductible traditional IRA for 1999.

Reason: Since their AGI exceeds $160,000, no deduction is allowed, period. In this situation, the husband or wife has only one option. They can contribute to a traditional *non-deductible* IRA up to $2,000 each.

Example 5: Husband has earned income of $35,000; wife has earned income of $15,000; and other income totals $6,000 for a combined AGI of $56,000 for 1999. Both are covered by employer retirement plans. Each spouse can deduct up to $1,000 each or $2,000 total for 1999.

Reason: Since their AGI is above the lower limit yet below the upper limit of the phase-out range for 1999, they would each be permitted to deduct up to 50% of the maximum of $2,000.

Be aware:

If your AGI is within the phase-out range of a deductible IRA and you want the deduction, be sure to contribute the balance of the $2,000 maximum to a Roth IRA.

Qualifying for Traditional Deductible IRAs
Filing Status: Single or Head of Household
For 1999

(Assuming earned income of at least $2,000) (Box A and B can be changed to reflect later years' phase-out ranges-- see Figure 3-1.)

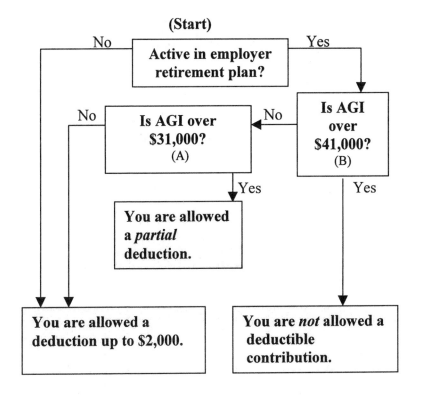

Fig. 3-3

<u>Qualifying for Traditional Deductible IRAs</u>
Filing Status: Married Filing Jointly
<u>For 1999</u>

(Assuming earned income of at least $4,000) (Box A and B can be changed to reflect later years' phase-out ranges-- see Figure 3-2.)

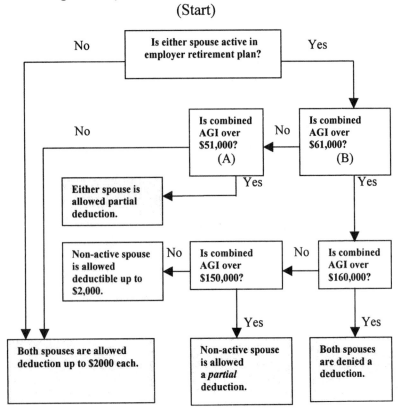

(Start)

Is either spouse active in employer retirement plan?

No   Yes

Is combined AGI over $51,000? (A)

Is combined AGI over $61,000? (B)

No

Either spouse is allowed partial deduction.

Yes   Yes

Non-active spouse is allowed deductible up to $2,000.

Is combined AGI over $150,000?

No

Is combined AGI over $160,000?

No

Both spouses are allowed deduction up to $2000 each.

Non-active spouse is allowed *a partial* deduction.

Both spouses are denied a deduction.

Yes   Yes

<u>Fig. 3-4</u>

CHAPTER 4

Choosing between a Roth IRA and a Traditional *Deductible* IRA Contribution

One of the most common questions for most individuals is whether to contribute to a traditional deductible IRA or a Roth IRA. This should be considered with as much calculation and analysis as possible because the outcome can be significant. This decision can have a material impact on how your lifestyle will be during retirement.

On the surface, it appears that choosing a Roth IRA over a deductible IRA may be the only choice. This is because tax-free growth in the future may outweigh the tax savings you receive today. There are a few instances in which choosing a traditional IRA may still be more favorable. So how can you be sure to choose the proper IRA with any degree of certainty?

To begin with, each individual has his or he own set of "variables." In other words, each individual will have to address four main factors that pertain to him or her. They are:

1. Current tax bracket

2. Retirement tax bracket

3. Rate of return on investments

4. Age and length of time before withdrawals

These factors will be used to project and compare values between the two types of IRAs and, ideally, to allow you to choose the best option. The bottom line is that you will be trying to achieve as much after-tax value or cash flow as possible. Keep in mind that no matter what method you use to do the projection work, you are not applying any science. As a result, your amounts will represent only approximations.

Inflation, future tax rates, rates of return, and your life expectancy will almost certainly have an effect on actual results. Did you know, for example, that prior to 1980 we had income tax rate brackets as high as 70%? The point I'm trying to make here is that no matter how sophisticated your projections or the calculators you use, there is always the chance that you could miscalculate what you expect to accomplish. This is not to say that an analysis based on certain assumptions couldn't be used as a *guide* to making the best choice of IRA as will be shown in the comparison illustrations of this chapter. The illustrations will show simplified results with varying assumptions. But before we begin to analyze any of them, let's examine the areas you'll have to become familiar with.

<u>Tax Brackets</u>

Generally speaking, if you expect your retirement tax bracket to be equal to or greater than your current tax bracket, a Roth IRA should work for you. For many, a higher tax bracket during retirement just won't be the case. The reason is that you will no longer be employed and your taxable income may be significantly reduced.

On the other hand, if you expect your retirement tax bracket to be lower than your current tax bracket, it may be that a traditional IRA is best suited for you. In this situation, you would be getting a tax deduction (using the traditional deductible IRA) while in your higher tax bracket and end up paying the tax when you fall into the lower bracket at retirement. This may be the choice for you.

In any event, it is recommended that you do some projection work on arriving at your retirement tax bracket.

No matter how you shake it, there is no escaping the fact that tax brackets play an important role in your projections and in choosing the better IRA.

<u>Getting a Handle on Tax Brackets</u>

How do you find out your current tax bracket? The easiest way is to ask the tax professional who prepared your last tax return. If you've done your own taxes or just want to do your own homework on the IRA issue, the following will explain a simplified process of finding it. It should be noted that calculating your tax bracket could become quite a bit more complex than is discussed here. Please consult your tax professional for more details regarding your individual situation.

Our tax rate structure for 1999 (the most recent release) is broken down by the type of "filing status" taxpayers use when filing their income tax returns. They are "single," "married filing jointly," "married filing separately," and "head of household." Each status carries its own tax rate structure as shown in the tax bracket tables below.

The starting point for identifying your tax bracket is your *taxable income*. Taxable income is the amount arrived at after deducting your itemized or standard deduction and your exemptions from your adjusted gross income. If that sounds a little scary, don't fret. You can simply look at line 39 on page 2 of your 1998 Form 1040. Looking there is fine for finding your current tax bracket as long as it represents a typical year. In a year in which there are unusual items of income and loss, you may be relying on an aberration, so be careful in a year like that. As I said before, this calculation is not a science.

The next step is easy; just look up your "taxable income" in the following tables.

1999 Tax Bracket Table for Married Filing Jointly

If taxable income is:	Your tax bracket is:
Up to $43,050	15%
$43,051 to $104,050	28%
$104,051 to $158,550	31%
$158,551 to $283,150	36%
$283,151 and over	39.6%

1999 Tax Bracket Table for Single Filers

If taxable income is:	Your tax bracket is:
Up to $25,750	15%
$25,751 to $62,450	28%
$62,451 to $130,250	31%
$130,251 to $283,150	36%
$283,151 and over	39.6%

1999 Tax Bracket Table for Head of Household Filers

If taxable income is:	Your tax bracket is:
Up to $34,550	15%
$34,551 to $89,150	28%
$89,151 to $144,400	31%
$144,401 to $283,150	36%
$283,151 and over	39.6%

Knowing your tax bracket at retirement

As indicated earlier in this chapter, it is important to know what tax bracket you'll be in during retirement so that the proper choice of IRA can be made

Taxable income during retirement years can be quite different from that of your earlier working years. Typically, wages or salaries no longer exist. This can mean a significant drop in taxable income for some people, and therefore a drop in tax brackets. This is not a good situation for choosing a Roth IRA.

To help you get a good idea on what taxable income (and your tax bracket) may be later in life, please refer to Worksheet 4-1 on page 70. This worksheet will assist you in arriving at taxable income both now and at retirement, which you will use to determine your respective tax brackets.

> ### *Be Aware:*
> Statistically speaking, women outlive men. This can have an effect on tax brackets since filing as a single can place you in a higher tax bracket.

Age and Length of Time before Withdrawals

When making the choice between the two types of IRAs, you must know the length of time or number of years your investments (contributions) will be at work for you. Your age will play a significant role in the decision process. The more years you have to invest, the better it will be for leaning towards the Roth IRA. When browsing through the contribution comparisons in this chapter (Figures 4-1 to 4-14), you can easily see why age and number of years to retirement are important.

Generally, the longer until retirement, the more attractive a Roth IRA is. Some of you, however, may be in a financial position to delay (or not need) withdrawals during retirement years. Those of you in that situation will be able to take advantage of better estate planning using Roth IRAs.

In Figures 4-5, 4-6, and 4-7 notice that the Roth IRA was not such a good idea. Age played a significant role in causing this comparison to fail to favor a Roth IRA. Sometimes these small differences favoring a traditional IRA can become even greater when you add the costs of losing certain tax credits and deductions (see Chapter 5 on conversions).

Be Aware:

There are instances in which individuals over age 60 may still find the need for a Roth IRA. One would be that you may not need IRA funds to live on, thereby allowing it to grow income-tax-free for your heirs.

Getting Comfortable with a Rate of Return

Historically, most benchmarks for projecting returns on investment have been in the area of 8% per year. For many years this percentage was used by nearly all financial institutions. It was a sort of "norm."

Today, in light of what has been happening in the stock market for the last 10 years or more, it has become more difficult to pick an average rate of return. Many mutual funds have experienced rates of return anywhere between 8% and 25% per year. I don't think we have ever witnessed anything like this in our history, and in my opinion, I doubt that it will continue.

This recent phenomenon makes the projection process quite a bit more difficult. During discussions with many of my clients in early 1998, I was surprised to hear that many of them (even those at or near retirement) were still completely sold on the idea of staying nearly fully invested in equities. They seemed to be mesmerized by their investment performances and weren't too concerned about a drop in equity values.

That kind of perception concerns me, but I suppose time will tell. Remember the saying: "Pigs get fat, but hogs get slaughtered." Be careful not to get too greedy; we may not see returns this generous again for a long time. This possibility should be particularly important to those of you at or near retirement since your time frame for taking funds out of your IRA will be sooner rather than later. If you fit this description, it may be that a more defensive posture for your portfolio is in order. This may

mean that your IRA portfolio should be weighted more in
fixed income investments.

In any case, it is only fair and conservative to use a rate
of return that reflects a historical norm. Hence, the
illustrations in this chapter will use an annual rate of 8%
to allow for a more realistic analysis when choosing your
type of IRA.

Comparisons of Deductible IRA vs. Roth IRA

In the following simplified illustrations, you will be
able to see the advantage of the Roth IRA over the
deductible IRA. As mentioned earlier in this chapter, if
your retirement tax bracket is equal to or higher than your
current tax bracket, a Roth IRA may be for you. By
looking at the following comparisons, you begin to see
why this is so in the majority of cases.   There are
instances where this may not be the case as shown in
Figures 4-5, 4-6, and 4-7. This is primarily true because
the length of time for your return on investments wasn't
long enough to recover all the tax savings you benefited
while in the 32% bracket.

Each illustration lists certain assumptions being used.
There is a comparison illustration for ages 30, 35, 40, 45,
50, 55, 60, and 65. Figures 4-1 to 4-7 reflect a current tax
bracket of 32% while figures 4-8 to 4-14 reflect the 19%
current tax bracket. The annual IRA contribution is
assumed to be made on the first day of each year. The rate
of return on investment for each comparison is 8%.

In order to keep things simple, I've only used the 19% and 32% tax brackets since the majority of taxpayers fall into these brackets. These tax brackets include a 4% state tax rate since most states would allow for the deduction of a traditional IRA and would tax a private pension. If you live in a state where these benefits are not taxed, you should be aware that your results would be slightly different. Again, these illustrations will represent only an estimate of your IRA values at the end of these time periods. Browse through them to find the one that resembles your age and current tax bracket to help you decide which IRA is suitable for you.

The term "tax savings account," as shown in the illustrations, is the amount a taxpayer saves when the traditional IRA is deducted on his or her tax return. In order for any of these comparisons to have any relational meaning, the tax savings amount is assumed to be put away in a separate interest-bearing account (a side account) yielding 5% per annum (in the real world, I doubt that individuals would actually do this).

The "tax savings account" is then added back to the cumulative deductible IRA value. This is to allow for an "apple to apple" comparison, if you will. After all, these dollars would not have been there if it hadn't been for the tax deduction.

For illustration purposes only, the "after-tax comparable values at retirement" are the amounts you would end up with if you were to withdraw all the funds in a lump sum and pay taxes at your respective rate. In reality, you would probably draw on these funds as needed and over many years, thus allowing your investments to continue to

grow and reap additional value (in both types) by doing
so. You would also have to consider the fact that if you
were in a traditional IRA, you would be *required* to make
withdrawals at age 70½. Accordingly, these illustrations
will serve only as a guide in helping you make a decision
on which IRA should be considered.

Contribution Comparison
Deductible IRA vs. Roth IRA
Age: 30
Rate of Return: 8%
Current Tax Bracket: 32%
Annual contribution: $2,000
Retirement age: 65
Tax savings from deductible IRA invested @ 5% taxable

Age	Cumulative Value of Roth or Ded. IRA	Tax Savings Account (after tax)
35	12,672	3,542
40	31,291	7,728
45	58,649	12,675
50	98,846	18,523
55	157,909	25,435
60	244,692	33,605
65	372,204	43,261

After-tax comparable values at retirement:

Roth IRA   **$372,204**

Deductible IRA @ 32% bracket   **296,360**
(372,204+43,261-119,105)

Deductible IRA @ 19% bracket   **344,746**
(372,204+43,261-70,719)

Fig. 4-1

Contribution Comparison
Deductible IRA vs. Roth IRA
Age: 35
Rate of Return: 8%
Current Tax Bracket: 32%
Annual contribution: $2,000
Retirement age: 65
Tax savings from deductible IRA invested @ 5% taxable

Age	Cumulative Value of Roth or Ded. IRA	Tax Savings Account (after tax)
40	12,672	3,542
45	31,291	7,728
50	58,649	12,675
55	98,846	18,523
60	157,909	25,435
65	**244,692**	**33,605**

<u>After-tax comparable values at retirement:</u>

Roth IRA   **$244,692**

Deductible IRA @ 32% bracket   **199,996**
(244,692+33,605-78,301)

Deductible IRA @ 19% bracket   **231,806**
(244,692+33,605-46,491)

<u>Fig. 4-2</u>

Contribution Comparison
Deductible IRA vs. Roth IRA
Age: 40
Rate of Return: 8%
Current Tax Bracket: 32%
Annual contribution: $2,000
Retirement age: 65
Tax savings from deductible IRA invested @ 5% taxable

Age	Cumulative Value of Roth or Ded. IRA	Tax Savings Account (after tax)
45	12,672	3,542
50	31,291	7,728
55	58,649	12,675
60	98,846	18,523
65	**157,909**	**25,435**

After-tax comparable values at retirement:

Roth IRA   **$157,909**

Deductible IRA @ 32% bracket   **132,814**
(157,909+25,435-50,530)

Deductible IRA @ 19% bracket   **153,342**
(157,909+25,435-30,002)

Fig. 4-3

Contribution Comparison
Deductible IRA vs. Roth IRA
Age: 45
Rate of Return: 8%
Current Tax Bracket: 32%
Annual contribution: $2,000
Retirement age: 65
Tax savings from deductible IRA invested @ 5% taxable

Age	Cumulative Value of Roth or Ded. IRA	Tax Savings Account (after tax)
50	12,672	3,542
55	31,291	7,728
60	58,649	12,675
65	98,846	18,523

<u>After-tax comparable values at retirement:</u>

Roth IRA   **$98,846**

Deductible IRA @ 32% bracket   85,739
(98,846+18,523-31,630)

Deductible IRA @ 19% bracket   98,588
(98,846+18,523-18,781)

<u>Fig. 4-4</u>

Contribution Comparison
Deductible IRA vs. Roth IRA
Age: 50
Rate of Return: 8%
Current Tax Bracket: 32%
Annual contribution: $2,000
Retirement age: 65
Tax savings from deductible IRA invested @ 5% taxable

Age	Cumulative Value of Roth or Ded. IRA	Tax Savings Account (after tax)
55	12,672	3,542
60	31,291	7,728
65	58,649	12,675

After-tax comparable values at retirement:

Roth IRA   **$58,649**

Deductible IRA @ 32% bracket   **52,556**
(58,649+12,675-18,768)

Deductible IRA @ 19% bracket   **60,181**
(58,649+12,675-11,143)

Fig. 4-5

Contribution Comparison
Deductible IRA vs. Roth IRA
Age: 55
Rate of Return: 8%
Current Tax Bracket: 32%
Annual contribution: $2,000
Retirement age: 65
Tax savings from deductible IRA invested @ 5% taxable

Age	Cumulative Value of Roth or Ded. IRA	Tax Savings Account (after tax)
60	12,672	3,542
65	31,291	7,728

After-tax comparable values at retirement:

Roth IRA   **$31,291**

Deductible IRA @ 32% bracket   **29,006**
(31,291+7,728-10,013)

Deductible IRA @ 19% bracket   **33,074**
(31,291+7,728-5,945)

Fig. 4-6

Contribution Comparison
Deductible IRA vs. Roth IRA
Age: 60
Rate of Return: 8%
Current Tax Bracket: 32%
Annual contribution: $2,000
Retirement age: 65
Tax savings from deductible IRA invested @ 5% taxable

Age	Cumulative Value of Roth or Ded. IRA	Tax Savings Account (after tax)
65	12,672	3,542

After-tax comparable values at retirement:

Roth IRA   **$12,672**

Deductible IRA @ 32% bracket   **12,159**
(12,672+3,542-4,055)

Deductible IRA @ 19% bracket   **13,806**
(12,672+3,542-2,408)

Fig. 4-7

Contribution Comparison
Deductible IRA vs. Roth IRA
Age: 30
Rate of Return: 8%
Current Tax Bracket: 19%
Annual contribution: $2,000
Retirement age: 65
Tax savings from deductible IRA invested @ 5% taxable

Age	Cumulative Value of Roth or Ded. IRA	Tax Savings Account (after tax)
35	12,672	2,144
40	31,291	4,758
45	58,649	7,947
50	98,846	11,835
55	157,909	16,578
60	244,692	22,362
65	**372,204**	**29,415**

After-tax comparable values at retirement:

Roth IRA   **$372,204**

Deductible IRA @ 32% bracket   **282,514**
(372,204+29,415-119,105)

Deductible IRA @ 19% bracket   **330,900**
(372,204+29,415-70,719)

Fig. 4-8

Contribution Comparison
Deductible IRA vs. Roth IRA
Age: 35
Rate of Return: 8%
Current Tax Bracket: 19%
Annual contribution: $2,000
Retirement age: 65
Tax savings from deductible IRA invested @ 5% taxable

Age	Cumulative Value of Roth or Ded. IRA	Tax Savings Account (after tax)
40	12,672	2,144
45	31,291	4,758
50	58,649	7,947
55	98,846	11,835
60	157,909	16,578
65	**244,692**	**22,362**

After-tax comparable values at retirement:

Roth IRA   **$244,692**

Deductible IRA @ 32% bracket   188,753
(244,692+22,362-78,301)

Deductible IRA @ 19% bracket   220,563
(244,692+22,362-46,491)

Fig. 4-9

Contribution Comparison
Deductible IRA vs. Roth IRA
Age: 40
Rate of Return: 8%
Current Tax Bracket: 19%
Annual contribution: $2,000
Retirement age: 65
Tax savings from deductible IRA invested @ 5% taxable

Age	Cumulative Value of Roth or Ded. IRA	Tax Savings Account (after tax)
45	12,672	2,144
50	31,291	4,758
55	58,649	7,947
60	98,846	11,835
65	**157,909**	**16,578**

After-tax comparable values at retirement:

Roth IRA   **$157,909**

Deductible IRA @ 32% bracket   **123,957**
(157,909+16,578-50,530)

Deductible IRA @ 19% bracket   **144,485**
(157,909+16,578-30,002)

Fig. 4-10

Contribution Comparison
Deductible IRA vs. Roth IRA
Age: 45
Rate of Return: 8%
Current Tax Bracket: 19%
Annual contribution: $2,000
Retirement age: 65
Tax savings from deductible IRA invested @ 5% taxable

Age	Cumulative Value of Roth or Ded. IRA	Tax Savings Account (after tax)
50	12,672	2,144
55	31,291	4,758
60	58,649	7,947
65	**98,846**	**11,835**

After-tax comparable values at retirement:

Roth IRA   **$98,846**

Deductible IRA @ 32% bracket   79,051
(98,846+11,835-31,630)

Deductible IRA @ 19% bracket   91,900
(98,846+11,835-18,781)

Fig. 4-11

Contribution Comparison
Deductible IRA vs. Roth IRA
Age: 50
Rate of Return: 8%
Current Tax Bracket: 19%
Annual contribution: $2,000
Retirement age: 65
Tax savings from deductible IRA invested @ 5% taxable

Age	Cumulative Value of Roth or Ded. IRA	Tax Savings Account (after tax)
55	12,672	2,144
60	31,291	4,758
65	**58,649**	**7,947**

After-tax comparable values at retirement:

Roth IRA   **$58,649**

Deductible IRA @ 32% bracket   **47,828**
(58,649+7,947-18,768)

Deductible IRA @ 19% bracket   **55,453**
(58,649+7,947-11,143)

Fig. 4-12

Contribution Comparison
Deductible IRA vs. Roth IRA
Age: 55
Rate of Return: 8%
Current Tax Bracket: 19%
Annual contribution: $2,000
Retirement age: 65
Tax savings from deductible IRA invested @ 5% taxable

Age	Cumulative Value of Roth or Ded. IRA	Tax Savings Account (after tax)
60	12,672	2,144
65	**31,291**	**4,758**

After-tax comparable values at retirement:

Roth IRA   **$31,291**

Deductible IRA @ 32% bracket   **26,036**
(31,291+4,758-10,013)

Deductible IRA @ 19% bracket   **30,104**
(3,1291+4,758-5,945)

Fig. 4-13

Contribution Comparison
Deductible IRA vs. Roth IRA
Age: 60
Rate of Return: 8%
Current Tax Bracket: 19%
Annual contribution: $2,000
Retirement age: 65
Tax savings from deductible IRA invested @ 5% taxable

Age	Cumulative Value of Roth or Ded. IRA	Tax Savings Account (after tax)
65	12,672	2,144

<u>After-tax comparable values at retirement:</u>

Roth IRA   **$12,672**

Deductible IRA @ 32% bracket   **10,761**
(12,672+2,144-4,055)

Deductible IRA @ 19% bracket   **12,408**
(12,672+2,144-2,408)

<u>Fig. 4-14</u>

69

Worksheet 4-1

For use in determining taxable income/tax bracket

	Now	At Retirement
Salaries/wages		
Interest/dividend income		
Business net income		
Rental net income		
Pension/IRA income		
Social Security taxable income		
Other income		
Total Income		
Less adjustments:		
Deductible IRA		
Keogh or SEP		
Health ins. (self-employed)		
1/2 self-employment tax		
Other adjustments		
Total Adjustments		
Adjusted Gross Income		
(Total income minus total adj's)		
Less:		
Itemized Ded.(or Std Ded)		
1999 exemptions		
(no. in family x $2,750)		
Taxable Income		
Tax Bracket		

(refer to tax bracket tables—page 49)

Caution: This worksheet is only a guide. Please consult your tax professional for additional help.

CHAPTER 5

Converting to a Roth IRA from a Traditional IRA

"A person doesn't know how much he has to be thankful for until he has to pay taxes on it."

Ann Landers

Undoubtedly this chapter will be the most important one for individuals who are contemplating converting (rolling over) their funds from a traditional IRA to a Roth IRA. For many, the mere mention of converting their IRA infers serious consideration and usually involves large sums of money. Thus, the decision to convert can be paramount to many. This chapter will attempt to give you insight on this complex subject while keeping it as simple as possible.

What Exactly is a Conversion?

Generally speaking, a *conversion* is when you direct the institution that holds your traditional IRA to change it (convert it) to a Roth IRA. This means that you have decided to leave your funds with the same trustee but want to change its character to a Roth IRA. A *rollover*, on the other hand, means that you are transferring your IRA funds from one institution to another (changing trustees) and in this case wanting it to be characterized as a Roth IRA.

The terms *rolling over* and *rollover* are synonymous with the terms *converting* and *conversion* when referring to changing the character of a traditional IRA to a Roth IRA. The tax code describes these so-called conversions/rollovers as *qualified rollover contributions*. We will view them as one and the same for purposes of moving funds to a Roth IRA.

Please note: To avoid being redundant, when I mention conversions, I am also referring to rollovers in most instances.

Any amount converted from a traditional IRA to a Roth IRA is treated as *distributed* from the traditional IRA and *rolled over* to the Roth IRA. The amount is generally includible in gross income for the year in which the amount is distributed or transferred from the traditional IRA (subject to a "four-year spread" for 1998 conversions unless the taxpayer elects otherwise). Therefore, the *taxable portion* of the conversion amount must be included in income, but since this also qualifies as a qualified rollover contribution, it will not be subject to an early withdrawal penalty.

Partial Conversions

Many individuals have several traditional IRA accounts. Some may include non-deductible contributions while some may be comprised of only deductible contributions. If you have traditional IRAs that include both deductible and non-deductible contributions, whether or not in separate accounts and whether or not you convert a particular one, you must aggregate them to determine what portion will be taxed upon conversion.

Let's say that you would like to convert one of your three traditional IRA accounts to a Roth IRA. For simplicity, each account has a current value of $20,000 ($60,000 total). One of these accounts includes $6,000 of non-deductible contributions. To figure the amount that is taxable upon conversion, you would need to subtract the non-deductible portion from the total of all the accounts to arrive at the taxable amount, and then convert it to a percentage. In this case, the amount taxable would be $18,000.

$$\$60,000 - 6,000 = \$54,000$$

$$\$54,000/60,000 = \textbf{90\% (taxable percentage)}$$

$$\$20,000 \times 90\% = \textbf{\$18,000 (taxable income)}$$

A special rule for rollovers is discussed later in the 60-day rollover rule.

Essentially, a conversion is deemed a *distribution* from your traditional IRA, *penalty-free* (but not tax-free) for the purpose of creating your Roth IRA. Unlike rollovers from one traditional IRA to another traditional IRA, the earnings and prior deductible contributions will be fully taxable. Be aware that these penalty-free conversions apply to any and all traditional IRAs that you wish to convert to Roth IRAs.

> ### *Be aware:*
> You are not allowed to do a conversion to a Roth IRA from any retirement plan unless it is a traditional IRA, including SIMPLE IRAs and SEP IRAs. This was clarified in the 1998 act.

In contrast to rollovers from traditional IRAs to traditional IRAs (where only one is allowed in a 12-month period), you can do as many initial traditional to Roth conversions as you like. This apparent difference allows you to convert as needed and permits you to do some tax planning, if need be. As an example, if you were to convert four separate traditional IRA accounts of $25,000 each in one year, you may push yourself into a higher tax bracket. The alternative may be to convert them over a two- to four-year period, thus keeping you in a lower tax bracket. More discussion of strategies will be covered at the end of this chapter.

The 60-Day Rollover Rule

Rollovers have to be completed within 60 days of receipt of funds from the original IRA. If you have decided to receive the funds from your IRA and make the transfer to the next institution yourself (not a trustee-to-trustee type), you must be careful not to miss the deadline for completing the rollover. If you do, it's as if you took a premature distribution and it will be fully taxed along with a penalty. There is no way to avoid the penalty unless you meet one of the exceptions (see Chapter 6). If you will be transferring the funds to another institution yourself, the paperwork can be cumbersome and time consuming. Be sure to act promptly.

To expedite the rollover process, I suggest doing a *direct rollover*. This is a trustee-to-trustee rollover. You will not handle the funds yourself. This method can also help to avoid unnecessary withholding of income taxes if not properly handled. Just be sure that you indicate in your paperwork that you do not want income tax deducted. You should not have taxes deducted if you will be rolling over the entire value of your IRA. This will allow you to make a full and complete rollover and avoid having to make up with the tax difference when getting the funds to the next institution.

If you do not intend to roll over the entire value, you may benefit by having taxes deducted, but be aware that a 10% penalty may also apply to the amount that is not rolled over. Authorizing the taxes to be withheld is a matter of so electing on the forms your trustee will provide you. Be sure to figure in the penalty tax amount (10% of the taxable amount not rolled over) if it will apply.

Why Do a Conversion?

If you can be relatively sure that you stand to gain a significant amount of tax-free money at a given point in time by taking some action today, would this be of interest to you? Of course it would! That is precisely what doing a conversion may mean to you. It is in your best interest to study your own set of circumstances to see if a conversion will benefit you. Refer to "Factors That Influence Your Decision to Convert" on page 88.

When considering converting your traditional IRA to a Roth IRA, you are in effect trying to determine whether paying income tax on the IRA's earnings and any prior deductible contributions *now* will make more economic sense than paying the income tax *later*. The time value of compounding money is at work here. Will it pay for you to cough up the tax dollars now in exchange for more tax-free dollars later? In most cases, yes! The fact that income tax brackets will have an effect on this decision emphasizes the importance of having equal or higher tax brackets at retirement (as was discussed in Chapter 4 relating to contributions).

Please note, as a rule of thumb, if you drop down in tax brackets at retirement by only a few percent (i.e., 31% to 28%), converting will begin to show advantages after about three years (see Figure 5-1). If you were to convert a traditional IRA when you're in the 28% federal tax bracket and fall into the 15% bracket during retirement, you may never see an advantage to a Roth IRA (see Figure 5-2).

$100,000 Conversion Comparison
Traditional IRA to Roth IRA

Rate of Return: 8%

Conversion-year tax bracket: 31%
Retirement tax bracket: 28%

End of Year	A After-Tax Traditional IRA Value	B Conversion to Roth IRA (taxes paid with outside funds)	Opp.* Costs (5% return taxable)	C Roth IRA Comparable Value
1	77,760	108,000	32,116	75,884
2	83,981	116,640	33,272	83,368
3	90,699	125,971	34,470	91,501
4	97,955	136,049	35,711	100,338
5	105,792	146,933	36,996	109,936

Fig. 5-1

* Opportunity cost is the amount of money you had to come up with (outside of your IRA) to cover the taxes upon conversion. This is considered money that could have been earning interest (I used a 5% rate) had you not done the conversion. Hence it became a cost for the opportunity to create your Roth IRA and should be deducted from the actual Roth IRA value in column B to make comparable sense.

$100,000 Conversion Comparison
Traditional IRA to Roth IRA

Rate of Return: 8%

Conversion-year tax bracket: 28%
Retirement tax bracket: 15%

End of Year	A After-Tax Traditional IRA Value	B Conversion to Roth IRA (taxes paid with outside funds)	Opp.* Costs (8% return taxable)	C Roth IRA Comparable Value
5	124,893	146,933	38,906	108,027
10	183,509	215,892	54,059	161,833
15	269,634	317,217	75,115	242,102
20	396,181	466,096	104,372	361,724
25	582,120	684,848	145,024	539,824
30	855,326	1,006,266	201,510	804,756
35	1,256,754	1,478,534	279,996	1,198,538

Fig. 5-2

* Opportunity cost is the amount of money you had to come up with (outside of your IRA) to cover the taxes upon conversion. This is considered money that could have been earning interest (I used an 8% rate) had you not done the conversion. Hence it became a cost for the opportunity to create your Roth IRA and should be deducted from the actual Roth IRA value in column B to make comparable sense.

By the way, I do not believe these scenarios to be that unusual, knowing that many conversions involve larger sums of money. If, for example, a married couples' taxable income is near the high end of the 15% federal tax bracket (1999=$43,050), any conversion income to be added in that year will cause them to pay tax on that amount at the 28% tax bracket (see tax bracket tables on page 49). These examples underscore the importance of making sure you are working with good estimates since a slight mistake in your estimates can render your analysis a lot less meaningful.

I am convinced that if you do not do enough research into tax brackets both in the conversion year and at retirement, you may be materially amiss on most projections. This is especially true for individuals nearing retirement. If you'll be working with a tax or financial advisor, be sure he fully understands what tax brackets you may be in.

As will be shown in the conversion comparison illustrations (Figures 5-3 to 5-8), it is almost always a good idea to do a conversion, especially when your retirement tax bracket equals or exceeds your current tax bracket. So why all the fuss over deciding to do a conversion to a Roth IRA? Shouldn't everybody do it?

Generally speaking, converting can make a lot of sense for a lot of people. The problem is that each individual must predict the future as it relates to a plethora of financial and tax data along with what your meaning of retirement is. This formidable task makes the whole prediction process a job for very detail-oriented people. In other words, it will be very subjective and time consuming. It's not as easy as choosing between a tax-free bond and a taxable bond in the marketplace. It may be that you will need to consult with your financial or tax advisor.

To help you understand what is at stake in predicting future data and making better use of a Roth IRA, I've listed the following conversion checklist. Each of the items may have an impact on whether or not converting is a good idea for you. If any of them apply to you, you'll need to be sure what effect, if any, they will have on your conversion or other financial planning.

Some of them can have very negative implications. An example of this is would be that you estimated a 32% tax rate bracket during retirement only to find out that it was really only 19%. How long your funds were in your Roth IRA will determine the cost of such a mistake. Not to throw water on your fire, but can you imagine what a blow a flat tax would be on a Roth IRA conversion? Remember, this is being discussed quite regularly on Capitol Hill these days.

Conversion Checklist

1. How long will you be able to leave Roth IRA funds invested before needing any of them?

2. Will you need funds earlier than age 59½?

3. Are you planning to leave all or part of your traditional or Roth IRA to heirs rather than taking withdrawals?

4. Do you have enough funds outside of your IRA to pay the tax cost of conversion to a Roth IRA?

5. Are you willing to invest in vehicles other than savings accounts?

6. Will you be able to predict a reasonable rate of return for your IRA investments?

7. Assuming no flat tax, will you have a good idea on what your retirement tax bracket might be?

8. Will estate planning become more important than retirement income planning?

9. Are you planning on buying a "first home"?

10. Will you be helping children or grandchildren with buying their first home?

11. Do you see yourself as providing financial help for the college costs of your children or grandchildren?

12. At what age will you be receiving Social Security benefits and what are the projected amounts? Will they be subject to income tax?

13. Do you currently take advantage of writing off real-estate rental losses on your tax return?

14. Are your children receiving any financial aid for education?

15. Do you itemize your deductions on Schedule A of your 1040 (for purposes of possible phase-out of deductions)?

16. Will you be qualifying for the Earned Income Credit?

17. Is your marital status going to change by the end of the year?

18. Do you think your 1040 can stand up to an IRS audit (for purposes of preventing the IRS from making upward adjustments to your AGI)?

19. Is your gross estate above or below the exclusion amount?

20. Will you lose out on the Lifetime Learning Credit during conversion year?

21. Will you lose out on the Hope Scholarship Credit during conversion year?

22. Will you lose out on the Adoption Expense Credit during conversion year?

23. Does your state tax retirement income from private retirement plans (IRAs)?

24. Have you taken the steps to avoid having to pay any estimated tax underpayment penalties?

25. Will you lose out on contributing to an Education IRA?

26. Will you name a non-spouse as beneficiary of your Roth IRA?

27. Do you foresee any large swings in your income?

The list is not all-inclusive, but it should help you be aware of other considerations when deciding to do a Roth IRA conversion. To the best of my knowledge, there isn't any software on the market that takes this kind of data into account. These questions are not intended to squash your plans for converting. The bottom line is to gather as much information on your situation as possible, assess the damages and the advantages, and then decide.

> **Be aware:**
> Prior non-deductible traditional IRA contributions will not be taxed in the conversion, so be sure you know your basis in them.

Who Can Do a Conversion?

To qualify for a conversion, your modified adjusted gross income must not exceed $100,000 in the year of conversion. When computing modified adjusted gross income for the purpose of determining that you have not exceeded the $100,000 ceiling, you do not take into account the taxable portion of the conversion amount itself. I guess that would make sense since many taxpayers might not otherwise even come close to $100,000 if that amount had to be counted. You are also not allowed to deduct any IRA contribution in the year involved for purposes of the $100,000 ceiling. I will refer to this modified adjusted gross income as AGI, as I did in Chapter 2, to keep the discussion simple and less confusing.

> **Be aware:**
> Amounts in retirement plans other than IRA types (401(k), profit sharing plans, etc.) must first be rolled over to a traditional IRA in order to be converted to a Roth IRA.

The same $100,000 AGI limit applies to both married individuals and those who file as single or head of household. This seems rather discriminatory to married couples since there are many areas in our tax code that distinguish different breaks for those who file as single from those who file as married (i.e., the exemption for gains on sale of principal residences allows married taxpayers $500,000 and single filers, $250,000). Where is the logic in our system? And why is it that the tax code does *not* allow married individuals who file separate tax returns to do a conversion or rollover to a Roth? Anyway, the following example will illustrate the foregoing $100,000 limit on AGI:

John and Mary Jones would like to convert all of their existing IRAs to Roth IRAs in 1999. Their existing IRAs are worth $50,000 (all taxable upon conversion). Their AGI before adding in the conversion amount, but after they both took a deduction for two traditional IRAs ($4,000), is $99,000. For tax purposes, their AGI is $149,000, but for conversion purposes, it is $103,000 ($99,000 + $4,000), thus making it impossible for them to qualify for conversion.

Be aware:

Married taxpayers filing separately are not allowed to do a conversion or rollover from a traditional IRA to a Roth IRA.

Due Date for Making a Roth IRA Conversion

Nineteen ninety-eight became the first year in which individuals could convert their traditional IRA to a Roth IRA, according to the Taxpayer Relief Act of 1997. These conversions can only be done *within* the calendar year. In other words, if you choose to convert to a Roth IRA for the year 1999, you will have from January 1, 1999, to December 31, 1999, to accomplish it. You cannot use the due date of your tax return (April 15) as you can for the contribution itself.

Roth IRA Conversions in 1998

As an incentive to have individuals do the conversion in 1998 (and a windfall for the Treasury Department), a special option exists. This option allows individuals the choice of electing to report the taxable conversion amount in the current year or spread the income equally over four years. Obviously, if you elect to spread the income over four years, you are basically getting an interest-free tax installment plan from the IRS. Who said the IRS isn't fair? This is a good deal if you can pull it off in 1998.

This option can also be very useful in doing some tax planning. In some situations, you may benefit by reporting all the conversion income in the current year when you know it is a relatively low-income year. On the other hand, spreading it over four years may keep you from jumping into higher tax brackets. You'll need to do a little homework in this case.

<u>Roth IRA Conversions after 1998</u>

There are perhaps millions of Americans each year who will be faced with the decision about going the Roth route. This is because millions of Americans each year are either changing jobs, taking early retirement or regular retirement, or needing to do something with their 401(k) plans, profit-sharing plans, etc. Since the planning opportunities of Roth IRAs offer so much, individuals will continue to consider converting, even without the four-year spread allowed in 1998.

If you missed doing a conversion to a Roth IRA in 1998, the reasons for doing it later are still very viable. The only difference (albeit a hard one to swallow) is the loss of the option to spread the income and pay the tax over four years. Putting it into perspective, if converting appears to be a good idea for you, missing out on the option to spread the tax may be nothing compared to what you stand to gain in the long run.

It may be wise to do post-1998 conversions for a couple of reasons. One, the tax-free compounding is still extremely advantageous, and two, you have your *own* option of spreading the conversion (doing a partial conversion each year) over as many years as you desire. This "self-spreading" can be utilized to keep you in a lower tax bracket and give you the time and ability to pay the taxes. Realistically speaking, many of these conversions involve large sums of money and the tax can be overwhelming. By doing partial conversions over several years, you may afford yourself the time to come up with the needed money to pay the tax from funds *outside* of your IRA funds, which is highly recommended.

Factors That Influence Your Decision to Convert

There are four main factors that have a direct effect on whether or not a conversion is suitable for you. They are the same ones mentioned in Chapter 4. For all the same reasons discussed in that chapter, you will have to become familiar with them. Again they are:

1. Current tax bracket

2. Retirement tax bracket

3. Rate of return on investments

4. Length of time before withdrawals

If you skipped over that chapter, I suggest you review it before proceeding.

Paying the Tax on Conversions

When deciding to do a conversion, you must always be aware that the tax burden can be quite substantial. Because of this, you will now be faced with an additional consideration. Where will the dollars to pay the tax come from?

The tax money can come from the converted IRA itself (which means there will be less left to invest), and any amounts taken to pay tax may be subject to early withdrawal penalties. The money to pay tax can also come from other personal funds such as a savings or money market account (recommended method). By using outside personal funds, you have more dollars working in a tax-free compounding environment, and you won't be paying the 10% penalty for early withdrawals. A 10% penalty is due on any tax-deferred portion of the traditional IRA withdrawn and not converted, unless an exception applies. You will see the benefit of paying taxes from outside sources in Figures 5-3 through 5-8.

Be Aware:

Because you are liable for additional tax when doing a conversion, you may be faced with having to make estimated tax payments to avoid penalties for underpayment of tax.

Undoing Conversions

What if you converted earlier in the year and later found out that you couldn't qualify or that it would have made more sense to stay in the traditional IRA? What if you converted when the value of your IRA was high only to find that if you had waited a bit longer to do the conversion, you would have saved thousands of tax dollars? These are all real-life situations. Many individuals were concerned whether or not the proposed regulations had definitively addressed the procedure for "undoing" a conversion or contribution. Questions remained in the minds of many as to how many times an individual could "undo" a previous conversion or contribution. In late 1998 the government issued IRS Notice 98-50 to address these concerns.

Basically it says if you do a trustee-to-trustee transfer to another IRA, you would have until the due date for filing your tax return (including extensions) to "undo" a conversion for the contribution year. This means that you could "undo" the previous conversion and have the funds (including all earnings) returned to your traditional IRA without any tax or penalty. This is known as "recharacterizing" the conversion and applies to contributions as well.

IRS Notice 98-50 (part of which is reproduced on pages 115-118) also clarified how many times you can "undo" or recharacterize a conversion. This notice will serve as an interim guide for those who will be involved with recharacterizing and reconverting their IRA conversions until December 31, 1999, or sooner if the IRS makes additional changes.

IRS Notice 98-50 essentially says that for a certain time you are going to be limited to one reconversion. The IRS notice was not intended for any "failed" conversions. This occurs when the taxpayer was not eligible for a conversion because of certain qualification reasons (i.e., failing the AGI test of $100,000). In other words, if you fail the test for qualifying, the "undoing" does not count towards the number of recharacterizations you are allowed to do. In fact, it is not to be considered a conversion at all.

This notice, however, did not mention that you needed to specify the reason for recharacterizing or reconverting conversions or contributions. Many people thought that this would be clarified, but it wasn't. Therefore, you do not need to explain your reason for doing your recharacterization or second conversion.

IRS Notice 98-50 was probably music to the ears of most financial institutions since it would relieve them of an ongoing and costly clerical nightmare.

Comparative Conversion Illustrations

The following conversion comparisons will attempt to give you an idea of what converting means in terms of after-tax values at the end of certain periods. They represent a simplistic approach and assume that taxes are paid at your respective retirement tax rate at the end of the period on the total value, as if it were withdrawn

You will need to look up the number of years you think the investment will be at work for you. For instance, if you did a conversion to a Roth at age 50 and wanted to know what your IRA values would be at age 65, you would simply go to the line representing the end of the year 15.

The illustrations all use $100,000 as the amount being converted. This amount is used because you can easily use a multiplier to arrive at your particular conversion amount and corresponding results. Let's say, for example, you would like to convert $150,000; you would simply multiply the year ending amounts by 1.50. If you convert $60,000, you would multiply year-end amounts by .60, etc. To illustrate, a $60,000 amount for an individual in the 19% tax bracket earning 10% for a period of 15 years (see Figure 5-5) would equate to:

After-Tax Trad. IRA Value = **$203,014**   (Column A)
($338,357 x .60)

Conversion to Roth IRA = **$250,635** (Column B)
($417,725 x .60)

Opportunity costs = **$20,679**
($34,466 x .60)

Roth IRA Comparable Value = **$229,955** (Column C)
($383,259 x .60)

There are three conversion comparisons for each of two tax brackets most commonly used, 32% and 19%. The 32% tax bracket is comprised of a federal tax rate of 28% and a state tax rate of 4% while the 19% tax bracket is comprised of a 15% federal tax rate with a 4% state tax rate.

For each of the two tax brackets, you will note that I've used three rates of return--6%, 8%, and 10%--to allow for a wider selection of investment vehicles. Figures 5-3 to 5-5 reflect results of being in the 19% bracket, both during the accumulation period and at retirement. Figures 5-6 to 5-8 represent the 32% bracket for both accumulation and retirement period.

There are two columns you'll need to focus on. They are:

<u>Column A:</u>

After-Tax Traditional IRA Value

And

<u>Column C:</u>

Roth IRA Comparable Value

Column A represents the value of a traditional IRA upon withdrawal after the taxes have been paid. Column A also represents what a conversion to a Roth IRA would look like if you were to pay the entire tax from the IRA account itself. I didn't show a separate column for this because the amounts would be exactly the same, assuming tax rates remained the same. A situation where this will show a difference would be one in which you did a 1998 conversion and spread the income and tax over the next four years.

Column B shows you the actual value of your Roth IRA (yes, it's all yours, tax-free) but will not be used in the comparisons.

Column C gives you the value of the converted Roth IRA when the "opportunity cost" is deducted. *Column C is to be used to compare the value with column A to appreciate the advantage of doing a conversion.*

A reminder once again: if you use any unconverted traditional IRA funds to pay the tax upon conversion, you may be subject to the early withdrawal penalty. This is not shown in the illustrations.

The illustrations assume that no further contributions are being made during the period, do not factor in inflation, and use currently available tax rates.

$100,000 Conversion Comparison
Traditional IRA to Roth IRA

Rate of Return: 6%

Conversion-year tax bracket: 19%
Retirement tax bracket: 19%

End of Year	A After-Tax Traditional IRA Value	B Conversion to Roth IRA (taxes paid with outside funds)	Opp.* Costs (5% return taxable)	C Roth IRA Comparable Value
1	85,860	106,000	19,770	86,231
2	91,012	112,360	20,570	91,790
3	96,472	119,102	21,403	97,698
4	102,261	126,248	22,270	103,978
5	108,396	133,823	23,172	110,651
6	114,900	141,852	24,110	117,741
7	121,794	150,363	25,087	125,276
8	129,102	159,385	26,103	133,282
9	136,848	168,948	27,160	141,788
10	145,059	179,085	28,260	150,825
15	194,121	239,656	34,466	205,190
20	259,778	320,714	42,033	278,680
25	347,642	429,187	51,263	377,924
30	465,223	574,349	62,520	511,830
35	622,573	768,609	76,248	692,361

* Opportunity costs (see footnote on page 77)

Fig. 5-3

$100,000 Conversion Comparison
Traditional IRA to Roth IRA

Rate of Return: 8%

Conversion-year tax bracket: 19%
Retirement tax bracket: 19%

End of Year	A After-Tax Traditional IRA Value	B Conversion to Roth IRA (taxes paid with outside funds)	Opp.* Costs (5% return taxable)	C Roth IRA Comparable Value
1	87,480	108,000	19,770	88,231
2	94,478	116,640	20,570	96,070
3	102,037	125,971	21,403	104,568
4	110,200	136,049	22,270	113,779
5	119,016	146,933	23,172	123,761
6	128,537	158,687	24,110	134,577
7	138,820	171,382	25,087	146,295
8	149,925	185,093	26,103	158,990
9	161,919	199,900	27,160	172,740
10	174,873	215,892	28,260	187,632
15	256,946	317,217	34,466	282,751
20	377,538	466,096	42,033	424,062
25	554,726	684,848	51,263	633,584
30	815,075	1,006,266	62,520	943,746
35	1,197,613	1,478,534	76,248	1,402,287

* Opportunity costs (see footnote on page 77)

Fig. 5-4

$100,000 Conversion Comparison
Traditional IRA to Roth IRA

Rate of Return: 10%

Conversion year tax bracket: 19%
Retirement tax bracket: 19%

End of Year	A After-Tax Traditional IRA Value	B Conversion to Roth IRA (taxes paid with outside funds)	Opp.* Costs (5% return taxable)	C Roth IRA Comparable Value
1	89,100	110,000	19,770	90,231
2	98,010	121,000	20,570	100,430
3	107,811	133,100	21,403	111,697
4	118,592	146,410	22,270	121,140
5	130,451	161,051	23,172	137,879
6	143,496	177,156	24,110	153,046
7	157,846	194,872	25,087	169,785
8	173,631	214,359	26,103	188,256
9	190,994	235,795	27,160	208,635
10	210,093	259,374	28,260	231,114
15	338,357	417,725	34,466	383,259
20	544,927	672,750	42,033	630,717
25	877,611	1083,471	51,263	1032,207
30	1,413,402	1,744,940	62,520	1,682,421
35	2,276,297	2,810,244	76,248	2,733,996

* Opportunity costs (see footnote on page 77)

<u>Fig. 5-5</u>

$100,000 Conversion Comparison
Traditional IRA to Roth IRA

Rate of Return: 6%

Conversion-year tax bracket: 32%
Retirement tax bracket: 32%

End of Year	A After-Tax Traditional IRA Value	B Conversion to Roth IRA (taxes paid with outside funds)	Opp.* Costs (5% return taxable)	C Roth IRA Comparable Value
1	72,080	106,000	33,088	72,912
2	76,405	112,360	34,213	78,147
3	80,989	119,102	35,376	83,725
4	85,848	126,248	36,579	89,669
5	90,999	133,823	37,823	96,000
6	96,459	141,852	39,109	102,743
7	102,247	150,363	40,438	109,925
8	108,382	159,385	41,813	117,572
9	114,885	168,948	43,235	125,713
10	121,778	179,085	44,705	134,380
15	162,966	239,656	52,839	186,816
20	218,085	320,714	62,454	258,259
25	291,847	429,187	73,818	355,369
30	390,557	574,349	87,250	487,099
35	522,654	768,609	103,126	665,483

* Opportunity costs (see footnote on page 77)

Fig. 5-6

$100,000 Conversion Comparison
Traditional IRA to Roth IRA

Rate of Return: 8%

Conversion-year tax bracket: 32%
Retirement tax bracket: 32%

End of Year	A After-Tax Traditional IRA Value	B Conversion to Roth IRA (taxes paid with outside funds)	Opp. Costs (5% return taxable)	C Roth IRA Comparable Value
1	73,440	108,000	33,088	74,912
2	79,315	116,640	34,213	82,427
3	85,660	125,971	35,376	90,595
4	92,513	136,049	36,579	99,470
5	99,914	146,933	37,823	109,110
6	107,907	158,687	39,109	119,579
7	116,540	171,382	40,438	130,944
8	125,863	185,093	41,813	143,280
9	135,932	199,900	43,235	156,666
10	146,807	215,892	44,705	171,188
15	215,707	317,217	52,839	264,377
20	316,945	466,096	62,454	403,642
25	465,696	684,484	73,818	611,029
30	684,261	1,006,266	87,250	919,016
35	1,005403	1,478,534	103,126	1,375,408

* Opportunity costs (see footnote on page 77)

Fig. 5-7

$100,000 Conversion Comparison
Traditional IRA to Roth IRA

Rate of Return: 10%

Conversion year tax bracket: 32%
Retirement tax bracket: 32%

End of Year	A After-Tax Traditional IRA Value	B Conversion to Roth IRA (taxes paid with outside funds)	Opp.* Costs (5% return taxable)	C Roth IRA Comparable Value
1	74,800	110,000	33,088	76,912
2	82,280	121,000	34,213	86,787
3	90,508	133,100	35,376	97,724
4	99,559	146,410	36,579	109,831
5	109,515	161,051	37,823	123,228
6	120,466	177,156	39,109	138,047
7	132,513	194,872	40,438	154,433
8	145,764	214,359	41,813	172,546
9	160,340	235,795	43,235	192,560
10	176,374	259,374	44,705	214,669
15	284,053	417,725	52,839	364,885
20	457,470	672,750	62,454	610,296
25	736,760	1083,471	73,818	1009,652
30	1,186,559	1,744,940	87,250	1,657,690
35	1,910,966	2,810,244	103,126	2,707,118

* Opportunity costs (see footnote on page 77)

Fig. 5-8

Strategies to Consider

On Reducing Adjusted Gross Income (AGI)

In order for you to qualify for doing a conversion from a traditional IRA to a Roth IRA, your AGI must not exceed $100,000. For many individuals, this would not be a problem, but for some who are near the threshold amount, some planning may be needed. Please read "Strategies to Consider" on pages 18-23 that pertain to reducing your AGI for qualifying for Roth IRA contributions. These same strategies can also be very useful for conversions.

Creating a Conversion Opportunity: Quit or Change Jobs

If you're thinking of leaving your employer and are a participant in the company retirement plan, quitting or changing jobs can create the "opportunity" for you to roll over your account balance to an IRA. From there, you will then be able to convert to a Roth IRA (assuming you qualify). My experience from speaking to many clients over the last nine months tells me that many of them wish they could handle the invested funds themselves so they can invest with more flexibility. Quitting one's job can be a method with which to accomplish that, although rather drastic.

Avoiding Paying Additional Income Tax on Social Security Benefits

Consider doing a conversion if you will be withdrawing IRA funds and you think your income during retirement will be at a level whereby most of your Social Security benefits will be subject to income tax. The following example illustrates this.

John and Mary Jones, both age 55 (in 1999), will be retiring at age 65 and will receive full Social Security benefits (estimated at $18,000 per year). Each was involved in a company pension plan and together will receive $40,000 in taxable distributions annually. Their current traditional IRA accounts total $60,000 (all taxable). These return 10% annually. If they were to convert the $60,000 in 1999 and pay the taxes due with outside funds, the results 10 years later would be as follows (assuming no inflation; currently available tax rates, exemptions, and standard deductions; and withdrawals of $15,000 per year from the IRA account):

Projected Income Tax for Year 2009

	With Conversion	Without Conversion
Taxable pension	40,000	40,000
Taxable Social Security	**10,250**	**15,300**
Taxable IRA	-0-	15,000
AGI	50,250	70,300
Standard deduction	-8,900	-8,900
Exemptions	-5,500	-5,500
Taxable income	35,850	55,900
Income tax (28% brkt.)	**5,378**	**10,056**

The *advantage* of converting to a Roth IRA before receiving Social security benefits, in this example, is **$1,414** in tax savings for 2009 ($15,300-10,250 x 28% tax bracket). Based on couples' IRA values at age 65, this can conceivably go on for many years!

Converting to Buy First Home

If you are buying a "first-time" home, consider converting your traditional IRA to a Roth IRA. The advantages are (1) you will not be subject to any early withdrawal penalty and (2) if you meet the five-tax-year holding period by the time you take a withdrawal for the purchase, you will not be subject to any federal income tax on amounts that would otherwise be taxable. The maximum lifetime amount for withdrawals such as this is $10,000.

This will also work fine if you are the parents or grandparents of the family member who is the "first-time homebuyer."

To avoid paying the penalty on this type of withdrawal, there are a few items you should become familiar with. The withdrawal must be for "qualified acquisition costs." These are basically any costs of acquiring, constructing, or reconstructing a residence, including reasonable closing costs. The property must also be a principal residence for you, your spouse, child, grandchild, or an ancestor of you or your spouse. In addition, the withdrawal must be used on the acquisition within 120 days of receiving the money and the individual buying the home must be a "first-time homebuyer."

A "first-time homebuyer" is basically anyone who has not owned a principal residence in the last two years (see page 121 for who qualifies). This means that the buyer does not necessarily have to be buying his or her very first home.

Converting Gradually

When contemplating a conversion, try to determine that you will not place yourself in a higher tax bracket than you will be in during retirement. If that is the case, consider doing a *partial* conversion.

This partial or "self-spreading" of the conversion income may also lead to preventing the phase-out of itemized deductions; loss or phase-out of real-estate rental losses; loss of Lifetime Learning Credit, Hope

Scholarship Credit, or student loan interest deduction; and possible loss of funding an Education IRA for children.

It is important for you or your advisor to be sure you are not too adversely affected by these phase-outs when your AGI falls within or exceeds them.

These phase-out amounts are listed in Figure 5-9.

Modified Adjusted Gross Income
Phase-Out Ranges
(For various tax credits and deductions)

	Single	Married/jointly
Education IRA	$95,000-110,000	$150,000-160,000
Lifetime Learning Credit	$40,000-50,000	$80,000-100,000
Hope Scholarship Credit	$40,000-50,000	$80,000-100,000
Student loan interest deduction	$40,000-55,000	$60,000-75,000
Adoption Expense Credit	$75,000-115,000	$75,000-115,000
Rehabilitation Investment Credit	$200,000-250,000	$200,000-250,000
Real-Estate Rental Losses	$100,000-150,000	$100,000-150,000
Exemptions Itemized ded.	$124,500-247,000 After $124,500	$186,800-309,000 After $124,500

Fig. 5-9

Converting for Estate Planning

If you have a substantial IRA and estate planning happens to be more important to you than retirement planning, a conversion should be considered. Unlike a traditional IRA, a Roth IRA has no required minimum distributions while you're alive. Thus, you are allowed to let the funds continue to grow and pass more money to your heirs *tax-free*. A traditional IRA would generally be taxable to the beneficiary.

Not having to pay income taxes does not mean that the value will avoid estate tax. A decedent's estate must include the total Roth IRA value in their "gross estate" for estate tax purposes.

An estate doesn't pay any estate tax if the gross estate is under a certain exclusion amount. Generally, if the estate exceeds the exclusion amount, it will incur federal estate tax. The basic exclusion amounts are:

Decedent Dying in:	Exclusion Amount
1998	**$625,000**
1999	**$650,000**
2000 and 2001	**$675,000**
2002 and 2003	**$700,000**
2004	**$850,000**
2005	**$950,000**
2006 or thereafter	**$1,000,000**

By the way, if you're not familiar with the tax rate structure for taxing estates, you may be surprised at how high it is.

60-Day Interest-Free Loan

If you will be doing an actual rollover to a Roth IRA and need a short-term loan (no more than 60 days) for any purpose, you will be able to use the funds for whatever purpose you desire during that 60 days. What makes this attractive is that you do not have to pay any interest on the money either.

One important thing to remember: if you do not meet the deadline for getting the funds to the next trustee (no more than 60 days after receiving the funds), you will probably have to treat the withdrawal as a premature one. This means that not only will you pay tax on the whole taxable portion, but the 10% early withdrawal penalty tax may apply also.

The date on which you will be deemed to have taken a premature distribution, in this situation, is the date on which you received the money. In other words, if you received the money on December 27, 1999, had intended to have it completely rolled over by February 25, 2000, but failed to do so, you would be liable for tax and penalty for the year 1999. This applies to partial rollovers as well.

Problems to Ponder

<u>Estimated Tax Penalties</u>

By making a conversion to a Roth IRA, you will more than likely subject yourself to the rules of making estimated tax payments.

Generally, the IRS requires you to make estimated tax payments when the tax due and owing is $1,000 or more at the time you file the tax return. If you fail to comply with these rules, you will be faced with a "penalty for underpayment of estimated tax." What this amounts to, essentially, is interest due on the underpayment portion. The rate is changed from time to time but is currently 8%.

Obviously, a Roth IRA conversion can easily place you in this situation. To give you an idea, let's say that your tax underpayment for the year of conversion averaged $6,000, and you did not meet any exception to the penalty. The amount of additional money due the IRS would be $480. This additional tax is not something you would normally be factoring in on your conversion analysis, so keep this in mind.

To circumvent this from happening to you, there are a couple of exceptions to the penalty. These are referred to as "safe harbor rules":

1. If you can keep your balance due the IRS under $1,000 by having enough withholding tax deducted from your paycheck or paying in

enough estimated taxes during the year, you will avoid the penalty.

2. For 1998, if you have paid in at least 90% of your total tax or have paid in 100% of the prior year's (1997) total tax, either by taxes withheld or by sending in estimated tax payments during the year, the penalty will not apply to you. Starting with the year 1999, this safe harbor rule will change for higher income taxpayers. If your prior year's (1998) AGI was more than $150,000 ($75,000 if married filing separately), you will have to pay in 90% of the current year's (1999) tax or 105% of the 1998 tax to avoid the penalty. For tax years 2000 and 2001, you will have to pay 106% instead of the 105%.

Problems with Required Minimum Distributions

Although the 1998 act clarified the issue on whether or not you had to include "required minimum distributions" to AGI for purposes of the $100,000 limit, Congress did not offer relief from this until the year 2005. Thus, if you are doing a conversion to a Roth IRA before the year 2005 and are receiving "required minimum distributions" from an IRA, you have to include those amounts in your AGI for purposes of determining eligibility.

IRS Audit Concerns

If the IRS audits you for a year in which a conversion to a Roth IRA took place and it revises your AGI above $100,000, you may have serious consequences.

If this were to happen, your Roth IRA would be disqualified. This may mean that your conversion from your traditional IRA will be deemed a premature distribution (to my knowledge, there is no relief for this). Consequently, the whole amount may be subject to the 10% penalty plus any interest.

The "big" problem is that it would be too late (60-day rollover rule) to roll the traditional IRA to another traditional IRA. Not only have you lost out on a Roth IRA, but you lost your traditional IRA as well!

If this happened for 1998 and you had spread the tax over four years, you would be taxed on 100% of the IRA rather than the 25% portion for that year. Adding interest and various penalties, this can be a devastating experience, so be sure your tax return is basically "audit proof."

Loss of Tax Credits and Deductions

By doing a conversion to a Roth IRA, it is conceivable that your AGI may get to a level where you may subject yourself to a loss of tax credits or deductions. As shown in this chapter, there are many such areas to be concerned with (refer to Figure 5-9).

The problem lies with the amount of dollars you would lose if one or more of these areas were to affect you. The amount of tax benefit lost would then have to be figured in the total opportunity cost in order for you to see any advantage to converting to a Roth IRA.

As an example, if you usually took the maximum deduction ($25,000) for real-estate rental losses and found out that it would be lost if you converted to a Roth IRA that year, how would your conversion now fare? Assuming a 32% tax bracket, the additional amount of tax cost would be $8,000. Depending upon the amount being converted and your time frame for having to withdraw IRA funds, this additional "opportunity cost" can have a material effect on deciding whether to do the conversion.

Effect on Education

If a conversion puts you in a position whereby your AGI is above allowable limits for obtaining grants or scholarships, the costs of such must be figured into your analysis. Sometimes the amount of benefit lost due to a conversion can be sizable and should therefore be factored into your analysis.

Losing out on other benefits, like the Hope Scholarship Credit or Lifetime Learning Credit may also need to be looked at. Some of these (credits, grants, etc.) could be lost in combination with each other, causing more concern for whether or not to convert. This can happen even when the amount being converted is relatively small. Be sure you or your advisor is aware of such financial effects.

Again, it pays to do some research in order to make a more informed decision.

Roth IRA May Be Vulnerable to Creditors

Since the enactment of the Taxpayers Relief Act of 1997, many states have not changed their statutes regarding whether or not the newly created Roth IRA is off limits to the claims of creditors. In the past, most states have passed laws regarding the protection of traditional IRAs from creditors' claims. This was primarily because state laws would reference specific IRS Code sections as being the type of asset that was exempt.

Since the 1997 act created a new code section on Roth IRAs and it wasn't immediately reflected in state statutes, it may be just a matter of time before states make the necessary changes. To be on the safe side, check with your state on this matter before making a conversion.

Getting Married before Year-End

If you were single when you decided to convert to a Roth IRA but by year-end got married, you could potentially have a problem.

As an example, let's say that Susie, single and age 30 with a projected AGI of $60,000, had converted her traditional IRA to a Roth IRA on March 1, 1999. On November 30, 1999, she married Jack, who will have W-2 earnings of $75,000 for the same year. Since their combined AGI will be over $100,000, they are both ineligible to do a conversion. Thus, Susie will now have to "recharacterize" her conversion back to a traditional IRA.

The reverse of this can also happen. In other words, you can have a married couple (with the same individual incomes as above) who were ineligible because their combined AGI exceeded $100,000. If they were to have their marriage dissolved before year-end, each of them would now be eligible for a conversion.

Not Converting Can Have Consequences

If you're sure you will not be depending on your traditional IRA during retirement, *not* converting to a Roth IRA may cause you to pay more taxes than you need to. This is because traditional IRAs do not have the same "luxury" as do Roth IRAs when it comes to distributions.

As mentioned in Chapter 1, Roth IRAs do not require you to take distributions at age 70½ while traditional IRAs do. Having to include income and paying tax from required minimum distributions can be avoided by doing a Roth IRA conversion. Be sure also to address this issue in your conversion decision and be sure that it fits with your overall estate planning.

IRS Notice 98-50

The text that follows is a reproduction of portions of IRS Notice 98-50. Like any IRS notice, its purpose is to give guidance on an issue until regulations are issued that are more specific.

PURPOSE

This notice responds to questions that have arisen regarding whether a taxpayer who has converted an amount from a traditional IRA to a Roth IRA may not only transfer the amount back to a traditional IRA in a recharacterization but also subsequently "reconvert" that amount from the traditional IRA to a Roth IRA.

TREATMENT OF CONVERSIONS

The question has arisen whether a taxpayer who has converted an amount from a traditional IRA to a Roth IRA may not only transfer the amount back to a traditional IRA in a recharacterization but also subsequently "reconvert" that amount from the traditional IRA to a Roth IRA. The proposed regulations do not specifically address this question, and the Service and Treasury are considering whether final regulations should permit reconversions under any circumstances. However, effective as of November 1, 1998, the interim rules set forth below will apply for 1998 and 1999. Any future guidance that either prohibits reconversions or imposes conditions on reconversions more restrictive than those imposed under this notice will not apply to reconversions completed before issuance of that guidance. If a taxpayer converts (or reconverts) an amount, transfers that amount back to a traditional IRA by means of a recharacterization, and reconverts that amount in a transaction for which the taxpayer is not eligible under the interim rules set forth in this notice, the reconversion will be deemed an "excess reconversion." However, any reconversions that a taxpayer has made before November 1, 1998, will not be treated as excess reconversions and will not be taken into account in determining whether any later reconversion is an excess reconversion.

A taxpayer who converts an amount from a traditional IRA to a Roth IRA during 1998 and then transfers that amount back to a traditional IRA by means of a recharacterization is eligible to reconvert that amount to a Roth IRA once (but no more than once) on or after November 1, 1998, and on or before December 31,1998; the taxpayer also is eligible to reconvert that amount once (but no more than once) during 1999. (Any conversion of that amount during 1999 would constitute a reconversion because the taxpayer previously converted that amount during 1998.) This rule applies without regard to whether the taxpayer's initial conversion or recharacterization of the amount occurs before, on, or after November 1, 1998, and (as indicated above) even if the taxpayer has made one or more reconversions before November 1, 1998.

A taxpayer who converts an amount from a traditional IRA to a Roth IRA during 1999 that has not been converted previously and then transfers that amount back to a traditional IRA by means of a recharacterization is eligible to reconvert that amount to a Roth IRA once (but no more than once) on or before December 31, 1999. In determining whether a taxpayer has made a previous conversion for purposes of these interim rules, failed conversion, as described in proposed regulations section 1.408A-4 (that is, attempted conversion for which the taxpayer is not eligible for reasons set forth in proposed regulations section 1.408A-4), will not be treated as a conversion.

Any excess reconversion of an amount during 1998 or 1999 will not change the taxpayer's taxable conversion amount (as defined in proposed regulation section 1.408A-8). Instead, the excess reconversion and the last preceding recharacterization will not be taken into account for purposes of determining the taxpayer's taxable conversion amount, and the taxpayer's taxable conversion amount will be based on the last reconversion that was not an excess reconversion (unless, after the excess reconversion, the amount is transferred back to a traditional IRA by means of a recharacterization). An excess reconversion will otherwise be treated as a valid reconversion.

Any conversion, recharacterization, or reconversion of an amount under this notice must satisfy the provisions of section 408A and the proposed regulations. For example, a taxpayer making a conversion or reconversion must satisfy the $100,000 modified AGI limitation of section 408A(c)(3)(B)(i) and proposed regulations section 1.408A-4, and a taxpayer transferring a contribution from one IRA to another IRA by means of a recharacterization must make the transfer on or before the due date for the taxable year of the contribution, as required by section 408A(d)(6) and proposed regulations section 1.408A-5.

In determining the portion of any amount held in a Roth IRA or a traditional IRA that a taxpayer is not eligible to reconvert under the interim rules set forth in this notice, any amount previously converted (or reconverted) is adjusted for subsequent net gains or losses thereon.

This notice is intended to clarify and supplement the guidance provided in the proposed regulations under section 408A and may be relied upon as if it were incorporated in those regulations. In accordance with the procedures for submitting comments on the proposed regulations, interested parties are invited to submit comments on whether final regulations should permit reconversions (and, if so, under what circumstances and conditions). Possible approaches to reconversions in final regulations might include providing that a taxpayer is not eligible to reconvert an amount before the end of the taxable year in which the amount was first converted (or the due date for that taxable year) or that a taxpayer who transfers a converted amount back to a traditional IRA in a recharacterization must wait until the passage of a fixed number of days (e.g., 30 or 60 days) before reconverting. Additionally, such approaches might include providing that an excess reconversion would be treated as a failed conversion that would be subject to the consequences described in proposed regulations section 1.408A-4 and that could be remedied as described therein.

Chapter 6

Withdrawing Roth IRA Funds

Ah, the joy of retirement and enjoying tax-free withdrawals from a Roth IRA! Isn't this the essence of why you decided to start a Roth IRA in the first place? Hopefully it will be a time in your life when you'll experience the fruits of your labor and a time in which you will appreciate the benefits of your Roth IRA.

Taking money out of your Roth IRA for various reasons and at various times can make a difference as to whether or not you may become subject to taxes and/or penalties. It is crucial that you understand the basic terms and guidelines.

The most important are:

1. Qualified distributions

2. Non-qualified distributions

3. The five-tax-year holding period for contributions

4. The 10% early withdrawal penalty on distributions

5. Taxing your distributions

6. The ordering rules for taking distributions out of a Roth IRA

7. Required minimum distributions

Qualified Distributions

One of the best ways to take money out of a Roth IRA is to take a "qualified distribution." This is when you are able to withdraw money both *tax-free* and *penalty-free*.

There are four instances in which a distribution (withdrawal) can be considered a qualified distribution.

The first I'll call the "ideal distribution." It is when you have met the five-tax-year holding period requirement and you are at least age 59½. In other words, you can withdraw money for any reason, at any time, in any amount and pay no tax and no penalty.

The next three instances I'll call "necessity distributions." These withdrawals will also have to meet the five-tax-year holding period and occur when they are for:

1. the **death** of the Roth IRA owner *or*,
2. the **disability** of the Roth IRA owner *or*,
3. a **"first-time homebuyer."** ($10,000 lifetime maximum.)

Definition of Becoming Disabled

You are considered disabled if you can furnish proof that you cannot do any substantial gainful activity because of your physical or mental condition. A physician must determine that your condition can be expected to result in death or to be of long-lived and indefinite duration.

Definition of "First-Time Homebuyer"

To qualify under this first-time homebuyer exception, a distribution must be used to buy, build, or rebuild a first home that is the principal residence of:

1. Yourself,

2. Your spouse,

3. Your child, or your spouse's child,

4. Your grandchild, or your spouse's grandchild,

5. Your parent or other ancestor, or

6. Your spouse's parent or other ancestor.

Note: The distribution must be used within 120 days of receipt of money.

Remember, a "first-time homebuyer" is anyone who has not owned a principal residence in the last two years. This means that the buyer does not necessarily have to be buying his or her very first home.

<u>Non-Qualified Distributions</u>

In the real world, as we all know, things don't always go as planned. There can be events that require you to take distributions (also referred to as withdrawals) somewhat earlier than anticipated. Withdrawing money from a Roth IRA before reaching age 59½ or before you have had the account for the five tax-year holding period can lead to taxes and/or penalties. These types of distributions are typically when:

1. you withdraw money **before age 59½** *or,*

2. you withdraw money for **"higher education expenses"** *or,*

3. you withdraw money for "**certain" medical expenses** *or,*

4. you withdraw money for **medical insurance premiums** when unemployed.

Definition of Higher Education Expenses

Qualified higher education expenses mean tuition, fees, books, supplies, and equipment required for the enrollment or attendance at an eligible educational institution. These expenses can be for only:

1. You,

2. Your spouse,

3. You or your spouse's children, or

4. You or your spouse's grandchildren.

Definition of Medical Expenses

These are medical expenses for which you did not receive any reimbursement, and the amounts total more than 7½% of your adjusted gross income for the year of Roth IRA distribution.

Definition of Medical Insurance Premiums

These are the medical insurance premiums paid by you in a year in which:

1. you lost your job.

2. you received unemployment compensation paid under any federal or state law for 12 consecutive weeks.

3. you made the withdrawals during either the year you received the unemployment compensation or the following year.

4. you made the withdrawals no later than 60 days after you have been re-employed.

The Five-Tax-Year Holding Period

The five-tax-year holding period pertains to both contributions and conversions (qualified rollover contributions). For regular Roth IRA contributions, the holding period begins on the first day of the individual's taxable year for which the *first regular contribution* is made or, if earlier, the first day of the individual's taxable year in which the *first conversion contribution* is made to the Roth IRA. The holding period will end on the last day of the fifth consecutive taxable year of the individual.

Keep in mind that you have until April 15 to make a *regular* Roth IRA *contribution* for the preceding calendar year, the same due date as your tax return. When doing a *conversion contribution,* you must complete the conversion *within* the taxable year you choose.

Since the law refers to "tax year" and not calendar year, this means that it is actually possible to wait less than five full years to meet this condition for regular contributions.

As an example, if you were to make a Roth IRA contribution for the tax year 1999 by the due date of April 15, 2000, you can conceivably meet the condition by taking a withdrawal on January 1, 2004. The five tax years would be 1999, 2000, 2001, 2002, and 2003.

When Does the 10% Early Withdrawal Penalty Apply?

Unless you meet one of the exceptions (pages 130-131), early withdrawal penalties for a Roth IRA *will* apply to earnings if they are taken *before* age 59½. It makes no difference that you met the five-tax-year holding period. The IRS just won't accept the idea of letting you get to your earnings before that age, without good cause.

Since all other distributions will fall under "qualified distributions" or for reasons of death, disability, "first-time homebuyer," certain medical expenses, certain insurance premiums for the unemployed, or for higher education expenses, the 10% penalty *will not* apply.

What about Taxes on Distributions?

Once again, if it's a qualified distribution, there is no tax (and no penalty), but if it's a distribution that falls *within* the five-tax-year holding period, the *earnings will be taxed.*

If your distribution from a Roth IRA is made *after* you meet the five-tax-year holding period but *before* age 59½ and qualifies as one of the following types of distributions, the earnings *will be taxed* (no penalty though).

1. For medical expenses that exceed 7½% of your AGI.

2. For medical insurance premiums paid by certain unemployed individuals (see definition on page 123).

3. For higher education expenses.

The Ordering Rules for Roth IRA Distributions

Now that we hopefully are clear about the rules for penalties and taxes, let's take a look at the order in which the IRS looks to taxing and penalizing the distributions from your Roth IRA.

Below I describe all the possible "elements" contained in a Roth IRA. This will help you understand why you need to keep good records if you will be taking withdrawals before they can become "qualified distributions."

Three basic "elements" of a Roth IRA are:

1. Regular Roth IRA contributions (the annual type),

2. Qualified rollover contributions (these are the type that you may have converted or rolled over to your Roth IRA) and,

3. Earnings from *any* contributions to the account(s).

Since you can have both traditional non-deductible IRA and traditional deductible IRA money in a Roth IRA account due to a conversion, there needs to be a further breakdown of qualified rollover contributions (item 2).

This means that you'll need to keep track of the "basis" of all traditional non-deductible IRA funds that exist within your Roth IRA account(s). This is because you can never be taxed or penalized on withdrawals of funds, which were from after-tax dollars in the first place.

As a result of the changes from the 1998 act, individuals are no longer required to keep separate accounts for conversion-type Roth IRAs and contributory-type Roth IRAs. If you do have more than one Roth IRA account, you will be treating them as if they were all one when applying the ordering rules on distributions.

Be aware:

The 1998 act made it clear that you do not have to keep separate Roth IRA accounts for purposes of keeping track of separate five-year holding periods. This means that the "first" date in which a contribution was made to a Roth IRA account (including qualified rollover contributions) will be the starting date for the five-tax-year holding period.

The order in which the IRS views distributions coming out of a Roth IRA account(s) is:

1. Contributions (your regular annual-type Roth IRA contributions).

2. Qualified rollover contributions (conversion or rollover funds) on a first-in, first-out basis. The first portion coming out of any of these types of distributions will be the taxable portion.

3. Any earnings since the inception of any and all Roth IRA accounts.

One example of applying the ordering rules to a distribution would be as follows:

John converted his traditional IRA with a value of $50,000 to a Roth IRA in 1999. It was comprised of $10,000 of non-deductible traditional IRA contributions, $20,000 of traditional deductible contributions, and earnings of $20,000. John also contributed $2,000 to a Roth IRA for 1999. If John, who is under age 59½ had withdrawn $43,000 of his funds (now worth $55,000 including $3,000 in earnings) within the five-tax-year holding period, he would have to pay $4,100 in early withdrawal penalties ($40,000 + $1,000 x 10%) and tax on $1,000. The breakdown would be as follows:

Roth IRA Elements in Order of Distribution	Value of Elements	Amounts Withdrawn	Amount Subject to Penalty(P) or Tax(T)
Regular Roth IRA contribution	2,000	-2,000	N/A
Qualified rollover contribution:			
Taxable portion	40,000	-40,000	40,000 (P)
Non-taxable portion	10,000	-10,000	N/A
Earnings	3,000	-1,000	1,000 (P&T)
Totals	55,000	53,000	41,000

Distribution Tables

The following tables show what types of distributions are taxable and which ones are subject to the early withdrawal penalty of 10%:

Roth IRA Distributions *after* Meeting Five-Tax-Year Holding Period and under Age 59½

Purpose of Distribution	Penalty Applies?	Tax Applies?	Penalty Applies to What?	Tax Applies to What?
No excludible purpose	Yes	Yes	Earnings	Earnings
Death	No	No		
Disability	No	No		
First-time homebuyer	No	No		
Medical expenses over 7½% AGI	No	Yes		Earnings
Insurance premiums of unemployed	No	Yes		Earnings
Higher education exp.	No	Yes		Earnings

Roth IRA Distributions *Not* Meeting Five-tax-Year Holding Period and under Age 59½

Purpose of Distribution	Penalty Applies?	Tax Applies?	Penalty Applies to What?	Tax Applies to What?
No excludible purpose	Yes	Yes	Earnings & *	Earnings
Death	No	Yes		Earnings
Disability	No	Yes		Earnings
First-time homebuyer	No	Yes		Earnings
Medical expenses over 7½% AGI	No	Yes		Earnings
Insurance premiums of unemployed	No	Yes		Earnings
Higher education exp.	No	Yes		Earnings

* Taxable portion of qualified rollover contributions (conversion contributions) that would normally have been included in income if the distribution were actually received and not rolled into a Roth

IRA. Essentially, these are amounts that represented the earnings and deductible portions of traditional IRA funds at the time of conversion.

<u>Required Minimum Distributions</u>

As discussed earlier in this book, you are not required to take any mandatory distributions with a Roth IRA as long as you are living. This is in contrast to a traditional IRA, which requires minimum distributions begin after reaching age 70½.

There are, however, required minimum distribution rules that you should be aware of that applies after a person dies. If you've named someone other than your spouse (a spouse is treated as the Roth IRA owner also) as the beneficiary, he or she will have to take distributions in one of two ways. First he can take distributions totaling the whole balance of the Roth IRA account by December 31 of the fifth year following your death. Second, he can also take distributions over his life expectancy, beginning in the year following the year of the your death. If he chooses the life expectancy rule, distributions need to begin no later than December 31 of the year following your death.

Not having to take distributions from a Roth IRA is one of the biggest advantages for those who will not be needing IRA funds during retirement. You can plan for more advantageous estate planning. By naming a child or grandchild as a beneficiary, you can eliminate a good deal of income tax and therefore leave a larger estate for your heirs.

If your grandchild was the beneficiary and he or she chose the life expectancy method for required distributions, can you imagine what the results of that might be? To illustrate, let's say you're age 60, don't need IRA funds during retirement, and have $100,000 in a Roth IRA returning 8% per year. If you lived to age 85, the value of your Roth IRA would be $684,848. The grandchild (age 35) would then be required to take distributions over his or her life expectancy. Since the grandchild is a non-spousal beneficiary and more than 10 years younger than the owner, he or she would be required to use certain rules (Minimum Distribution Incidental Benefit rules). Even with the rules, the value becomes quite large (well into seven figures) and the distributions significant. This shows you how impressive tax-free compounding can be.

Will You Need to Withdraw IRA Funds at Retirement?

We've all heard it before: Americans don't save enough for their retirement and many are not covered by employer retirement plans. Social Security benefits alone will not suffice for retirement (see Figure 6-1). The scenario is typical. This is one of the reasons why most individuals *will* have a need for additional funds during retirement. Do your homework now. Try to determine the amount of money needed during your retirement years. The more informed you are now, the better your planning will be.

Social Security Average Monthly Benefits

Period	Retired Worker	Spouse of Worker
1985	$478.62	$246.28
1990	602.56	311.18
1995	719.80	370.43
1996	744.96	383.50
1997	764.98	393.05

Source: Social Security Administration

Fig. 6-1

Unless you're in tune with your monthly or annual budget, the amount of cash you're really shelling out annually may surprise you. This was the case with many of my clients. With the help of Worksheets 6-1 and 6-2 (pages 148-149), you will get a good idea of your current and retirement cash flow needs and be able to determine the amount of money needed to fulfill your retirement lifestyle. You should note that, by doing this exercise, you might find that some budget trimming is in order. Take the time to get as accurate as possible since the results will be crucial in sizing up the amount of withdrawals you will be taking from your IRA account.

Since inflation is a force to reckon with, I've included a table (Figure 6-2) to help you determine what future expenses may be. For example, if your current food costs are running $4,800 a year, 10 years from now they may be $6,432. You simply multiply the cost today times the multiplier in the table for the number of years and rate of inflation you're projecting. In this case, I've used an inflation rate of 3% for a period of 10 years, which is a multiplier of 1.34.

Inflation Multiplier Table
Inflation rates

Years	3%	5%	7%
5	1.16	1.28	1.40
10	1.34	1.63	1.97
15	1.56	2.08	2.76
20	1.81	2.65	3.87
25	2.09	3.39	5.43

Fig. 6-2

For those of you who think you can either minimize or delay withdrawals from your IRA during retirement, it is just as important for you to know your cash flow needs. You may be in a position to allow your Roth IRA funds to be invested for a longer period, thereby having your funds grow even more, and tax-free! This is now possible with Roth IRAs because you do not have to take any required minimum distributions at age 70½. Don't overlook this advantage. Most retirees should first consider using funds outside of Roth IRA accounts to cover day-to-day cash flow needs.

Food for Thought . . .

Did you know that it takes 12 to 15 years for people receiving full Social Security benefits (age 65) to come out better than those people taking early retirement (age 62) with reduced Social Security benefits?

Did you know that, as of 1996, Social Security benefits provided 50% or more of total income for 66% of the beneficiaries? Social Security benefits provided 90% or more of total income for almost one-third of the beneficiaries and was the only source of income for 18% of those.

How Long Will Your Roth IRA Last When Distributions Begin?

Factors such as your financial needs during retirement, the size of your Roth IRA account(s), rate of return, and whether or not you'll continue to fund your Roth IRA will determine how long your funds will really last.

I've assembled various illustrations in Figures 6-3 to 6-12 to give you an idea about how your account may look using various parameters. Each of the illustrations uses a conservative 6% return on investments (to be prudent). There are three annual withdrawal amounts, $12,000, $24,000, and $36,000, for each of the two tax brackets (19% and 32%). As mentioned earlier, these rates include a 4% state income tax. The amounts used under "Annual Withdrawal from Traditional IRA" include sufficient amounts to cover the income tax, but the net amount would still be equal to a Roth IRA withdrawal. Other assumptions are:

- No further contributions are being made.
- No inflation is factored in for withdrawals.
- All annual withdrawals occur on the first day of each year.
- Current tax rates are being used.

Since it would be very difficult to represent the unlimited number of withdrawal scenarios, the following illustrations will serve as guidance for those whose funds and needs are similar. You should at least be able to get an idea on how long your Roth IRA nest egg will carry you during a withdrawal period.

If, as shown in some of the illustrations, your Roth IRA account balance continues to grow, you'll at least know that you may need to take a harder look at your estate planning.

Withdrawal Comparisons
Starting Balance: $100,000

$12,000 Annual Withdrawal

6% Return on investments
32% Tax bracket

End of Year	Annual Withdrawal Traditional IRA	Balance of Traditional IRA	Annual Withdrawal Roth IRA	Balance of Roth IRA
1	17,647	87,294	12,000	93,280
2	17,647	73,826	12,000	86,157
3	17,647	59,550	12,000	78,606
4	17,647	44,417	12,000	70,603
5	17,647	28,376	12,000	62,119
6	17,647	11,373	12,000	53,126
7	11,373	0	12,000	43,593
8			12,000	33,489
9			12,000	22,778
10			12,000	11,425
11			11,425	0

Traditional IRA lasts **6.64** years
Roth IRA lasts **10.95** years

Fig. 6-3

Withdrawal Comparisons
Starting Balance: $250,000

$12,000 Annual Withdrawal

6% Return on investments
32% Tax bracket

End of Year	Annual Withdrawal Traditional IRA	Balance of Traditional IRA	Annual Withdrawal Roth IRA	Balance of Roth IRA
1	17,647	246,294	12,000	252,280
2	17,647	242,366	12,000	254,697
3	17,647	238,202	12,000	257,259
4	17,647	233,788	12,000	259,974
5	17,647	229,110	12,000	262,853
6	17,647	224,151	12,000	265,904
7	17,647	218,894	12,000	269,138
8	17,647	213,322	12,000	272,566
9	17,647	207,415	12,000	276,200
10	17,647	201,154	12,000	280,052
15	17,647	163,743	12,000	303,069
20	17,647	113,679	12,000	333,871
25	17,647	46,682	12,000	375,091
28	13,918	0	12,000	406,244

Traditional IRA lasts **27.78** years
Roth IRA **continues** to grow

Fig. 6-4

Withdrawal Comparisons
Starting Balance: $100,000

$24,000 Annual Withdrawal

6% Return on investments
32% Tax bracket

End of Year	Annual Withdrawal Traditional IRA	Balance of Traditional IRA	Annual Withdrawal Roth IRA	Balance of Roth IRA
1	35,294	68,588	24,000	80,560
2	35,294	35,292	24,000	59,954
3	35,292	0	24,000	38,111
4			24,000	14,957
5			14,957	0

Traditional IRA lasts **2.99** years
Roth IRA lasts **4.62** years

Fig. 6-5

Withdrawal Comparisons
Starting Balance: $250,000

$24,000 Annual Withdrawal

6% Return on investments
32% Tax bracket

End of Year	Annual Withdrawal Traditional IRA	Balance of Traditional IRA	Annual Withdrawal Roth IRA	Balance of Roth IRA
1	35,294	227,588	24,000	239,560
2	35,294	203,832	24,000	228,494
3	35,294	178,650	24,000	216,763
4	35,294	151,958	24,000	204,329
5	35,294	123,664	24,000	191,149
6	35,294	93,672	24,000	177,178
7	35,294	61,880	24,000	162,368
8	35,294	28,182	24,000	146,670
9	28,182	0	24,000	130,031
10			24,000	112,393
11			24,000	93,696
12			24,000	73,787
13			24,000	52,870
14			24,000	30,603
15			24,,000	6,999
16			6,999	0

Traditional IRA lasts **8.80** years
Roth IRA lasts **15.29** years

Fig.6-6

Withdrawal Comparisons
Starting Balance: $500,000

$24,000 Annual Withdrawal

6% Return on investments
32% Tax bracket

End of Year	Annual Withdrawal Traditional IRA	Balance of Traditional IRA	Annual Withdrawal Roth IRA	Balance of Roth IRA
1	35,294	492,588	24,000	504,560
2	35,294	484,732	24,000	509,394
3	35,294	476,404	24,000	514,517
4	35,294	467,577	24,000	519,948
5	35,294	458,220	24,000	525,705
6	35,294	448,301	24,000	531,807
7	35,294	437,788	24,000	538,276
8	35,294	426,644	24,000	545,132
9	35,294	414,831	24,000	552,400
10	35,294	402,309	24,000	560,104
15	35,294	327,487	24,000	606,138
20	35,294	227,358	24,000	667,742
25	35,294	93,364	24,000	750,182
28	27,836	0	24,000	812,488

Traditional IRA lasts **27.79** years
Roth IRA **continues** to grow

Fig. 6-7

Withdrawal Comparisons
Starting Balance: $500,000

$36,000 Annual Withdrawal

6% Return on investments
32% Tax bracket

End of Year	Annual Withdrawal Traditional IRA	Balance of Traditional IRA	Annual Withdrawal Roth IRA	Balance of Roth IRA
1	52,941	473,883	36,000	491,840
2	52,941	446,198	36,000	483,190
3	52,941	416,852	36,000	474,022
4	52,941	385,746	36,000	464,303
5	52,941	352,773	36,000	454,001
6	52,941	317,822	36,000	443,081
7	52,941	280,774	36,000	431,506
8	52,941	241,503	36,000	419,237
9	52,941	199,876	36,000	406,231
10	52,941	155,751	36,000	392,445
11	52,941	108,979	36,000	377,831
12	52,941	59,400	36,000	362,341
13	52,941	6,847	36,000	345,922
14	6,847	0	36,000	328,517
15			36,000	310,068
20			36,000	199,830
25			36,000	52,306
27			17,284	0

Traditional IRA lasts **13.13** years
Roth IRA lasts **26.48** years
Fig. 6-8

Withdrawal Comparisons
Starting Balance: $100,000

$12,000 Annual Withdrawal

6% Return on investments
19% Tax bracket

End of Year	Annual Withdrawal Traditional IRA	Balance of Traditional IRA	Annual Withdrawal Roth IRA	Balance of Roth IRA
1	14,815	90,296	12,000	93,280
2	14,815	80,010	12,000	86,157
3	14,815	69,107	12,000	78,606
4	14,815	57,549	12,000	70,603
5	14,815	45,298	12,000	62,119
6	14,815	32,312	12,000	53,126
7	14,815	18,547	12,000	43,593
8	14,815	3,956	12,000	33,489
9	3,956	0	12,000	22,778
10			12,000	11,425
11			11,425	0

Traditional IRA lasts **8.27** years
Roth IRA lasts **10.95** years

Fig. 6-9

Withdrawal Comparisons
Starting Balance: $250,000

$12,000 Annual Withdrawal

6% Return on investments
19% Tax bracket

End of Year	Annual Withdrawal Traditional IRA	Balance of Traditional IRA	Annual Withdrawal Roth IRA	Balance of Roth IRA
1	14,815	249,296	12,000	252,280
2	14,815	248,550	12,000	254,697
3	14,815	247,759	12,000	257,259
4	14,815	246,921	12,000	259,974
5	14,815	246,032	12,000	262,853
6	14,815	245,090	12,000	265,904
7	14,815	244,092	12,000	269,138
8	14,815	243,033	12,000	272,566
9	14,815	241,911	12,000	276,200
10	14,815	240,722	12,000	280,052
15	14,815	233,616	12,000	303,069
20	14,815	224,107	12,000	333,871
25	14,815	211,381	12,000	375,091
30	14,815	194,351	12,000	430,253
35	14,815	171,561	12,000	504,071
54	4,354	0	12,000	1,095,691

Traditional IRA lasts **53.29** years
Roth IRA **continues** to grow

Fig. 6-10

Withdrawal Comparisons
Starting Balance: $250,000

$24,000 Annual Withdrawal

6% Return on investments
19% Tax bracket

End of Year	Annual Withdrawal Traditional IRA	Balance of Traditional IRA	Annual Withdrawal Roth IRA	Balance of Roth IRA
1	29,630	233,592	24,000	239,560
2	29,630	216,200	24,000	228,494
3	29,630	197,764	24,000	216,763
4	29,630	178,222	24,000	204,329
5	29,630	157,508	24,000	191,149
6	29,630	135,550	24,000	177,178
7	29,630	112,276	24,000	162,368
8	29,630	87,604	24,000	146,670
9	29,630	61,453	24,000	130,031
10	29,630	33,732	24,000	112,393
11	29,630	4,348	24,000	93,696
12	4,348	0	24,000	73,787
13			24,000	52,870
14			24,000	30,603
15			24,000	6,999
16			6,900	0

Traditional IRA lasts **11.15** years
Roth IRA lasts **15.29** years

Fig. 6-11

Withdrawal Comparisons
Starting Balance: $500,000
$36,000 Annual Withdrawal
6% Return on investments
19% Tax bracket

End of Year	Annual Withdrawal Traditional IRA	Balance of Traditional IRA	Annual Withdrawal Roth IRA	Balance of Roth IRA
1	44,444	482,889	36,000	491,840
2	44,444	464,752	36,000	483,190
3	44,444	445,527	36,000	474,022
4	44,444	425,148	36,000	464,303
5	44,444	403,546	36,000	454,001
6	44,444	380,648	36,000	443,081
7	44,444	356,376	36,000	431,506
8	44,444	330,648	36,000	419,237
9	44,444	303,376	36,000	406,231
10	44,444	274,468	36,000	392,445
11	44,444	243,826	36,000	377,831
12	44,444	211,345	36,000	362,341
13	44,444	176,915	36,000	345,922
14	44,444	140,419	36,000	328,517
15	44,444	101,733	36,000	310,068
16	44,444	60,727	36,000	290,512
17	44,444	17,260	36,000	269,783
18	17,260	0	36,000	247,810
20			36,000	199,830
25			36,000	52,306
27			17,284	0

Traditional IRA lasts **17.39** years
Roth IRA lasts **26.48** years
Fig. 6-12

Worksheet 6-1

For use in determining annual cash flow needs

Annual Cash Outlay:	Now	At Retirement
Mortgage/rent		
Real-estate taxes		
Utilities		
Telephone/cable		
Homeowner's insurance		
Water/sewer		
Home maint./repairs		
Food/dining out		
Car payments		
Car fuel/oil/repairs		
Car licenses		
Car insurance		
Clothing		
Personal care/hair		
Health insurance		
Life insurance		
Unreimb. medical exp.		
Eye care		
Entertainment		
Vacation expenses		
Family gifts (various)		
Charitable donations		
Income taxes (state/fed)		
Pet care		
Other installment debt		
Education/health club		
Other expenses		
Total Annual Outlay		

Worksheet 6-2

Net Annual Income

	Now	At Retirement
Net wages-you		
Net wages-spouse		
Interest income		
Dividend income		
Annuity income		
Capital gain distributions		
Rental property income		
Net income-business		
Other income		
Social Security-you		
Social Security-spouse		
Pension income-you		
Pension income-spouse		

Total Net Annual Income _____

(Compare these totals with *total annual outlays* on Worksheet 6-1 to see if you'll meet your desired cash flow needs.**)**

Chapter 7

Questions and Answers

Question: Do you need to maintain separate accounts for Roth IRA contributions and Roth IRA conversions?

Answer: No, all Roth IRA accounts are treated as one account. It makes no difference that you maintain them separately.

Question: Will I be charged a fee for doing a conversion?

Answer: While many do not, I understand that some institutions now charge a nominal fee of about $10.

Question: If I am already participating in a SEP (Simplified Employee Pension) or SIMPLE (Savings Incentive Match Plan for Employees) IRA, will I be eligible to contribute to a Roth IRA?

Answer: Assuming you qualify otherwise, you can also contribute to a Roth IRA. This was clarified in the 1998 act.

Question: Can I contribute to a Roth IRA for my child?

Answer: Yes, as long as your child has enough earned income to qualify.

Question: If I contribute the maximum $2,000 to my child's Roth IRA, will I also be able to fund an Education IRA for him?

Answer: Yes, the Education IRA is not counted towards the maximum contribution allowed for a Roth IRA.

Question: Is it still a good idea for me to do a conversion after 1998?

Answer: If you know that you will benefit in the long term, the answer is absolutely yes. If it will be difficult to pay the taxes in one year, consider doing partial conversions.

Question: If I make a small Roth IRA contribution ($100), will this be enough to start the five-year holding period so I can begin taking tax-free withdrawals when I reach age 59½?

Answer: Yes, the tax code does not define the amount of contribution needed.

Question: Will my Roth IRA be subject to estate taxes at my death?

Answer: Yes, it is included in your estate for estate tax purposes. However, it will not be subject to income taxes if the Roth IRA account meets the five-year holding period.

Question: Will I be able to contribute to a Roth IRA once I am retired?

Answer: You can contribute to a Roth IRA as long as you have earned income and you do not exceed your AGI limit.

Question: Will I be able to contribute to a Roth IRA if I already contribute to my 401(k) plan?

Answer: Yes, as long as you don't exceed your AGI limit.

Question: If I do a conversion to a Roth IRA, will I be subject to making quarterly estimated tax payments?

Answer: The tax law for making estimated tax payments did not change with the addition of the new Roth IRA and therefore you will need to determine whether the distribution amount added to your income qualifies you for having to make estimated tax payments.

Question: I heard there are required minimum distributions with a Roth IRA. Is that true?

Answer: There are no required distributions while you are alive, but there are upon your death if the beneficiary is other than your spouse.

Question: What will I do if I later find out that I didn't qualify for a Roth IRA contribution or conversion?

Answer: You can always "undo" a conversion if you failed the AGI limitation. You can also withdraw your Roth IRA contribution as if you never made it. The due date for accomplishing these is the due date of the tax return (including extensions).

Question: Can I roll over a distribution from my 401(k) plan into a Roth IRA?

Answer: No, you must first roll it over to a traditional IRA. You will then be able to do a conversion to a Roth IRA from there.

Question: Is it true that I may have to pay taxes on Social Security benefits when I start taking traditional IRA withdrawals?

Answer: That all depends on your income. If adding the distribution to your income puts you over certain dollar amounts, your benefits may well be taxed.

Question: Isn't the Roth IRA good for everyone?

Answer: It is advantageous for many individuals. Because there are many variables to be considered, an analysis must be performed to determine if it will work for you.

Index

choosing between Roth and traditional deductible IRAs, 45-70
college expenses, see higher education
commissions, and earned income, 9
comparing Roth and traditional IRAs, *see* choosing between Roth and traditional deductible IRAs
constructive receipt of income, 19
contribution comparisons, 56-69
contributions to IRAs
    allowable
        for head of household filers, 10-11, 14, 15, 34
        for married (filing jointly) filers, 12-14, 16, 39
        for married (filing separately) filers, 12-14, 17, 85
        for single filers, 10-11, 14, 15, 34
    due dates for, 5-6, 86, 124
    excess, 14
    maximum, 6, 12, 14-17, 37
    and order of withdrawals, 126-128
conversions
    comparisons of, 76-83, 88, 91-100, 114
    due dates for, 6, 86, 124
    and estate planning, 107
    failed, 90, 117
    from traditional to Roth IRAs, 28, 71-74, 87-88
    and income limits, 19, 101
    partial, 72-74, 87, 104-105
    qualifying for, 84-85, 90
    recharacterizing, 89-91, 115-118
    and reconversions, 115-118
    self-spreading of, 87, 104-105
    tax cost of, 76, 81, 87, 88-89, 93, 94, 153
    taxable portions of, 72, 73-74, 84
    undoing, *see* conversions, recharacterizing
creation of Roth IRA by Congress, 1-2, 3
creditors and IRAs, 113

D

deadlines, *see* due dates
death of IRA owner, 120, 125, 130-131, 153
deductible IRAs, *see* traditional IRAs, deductible contributions to
deferral of taxes, 2-3, 18, 19
delayed billing, 21

popularity of, 1, 3-4, 7
and taxable distributions, 125-126, 129-131
withdrawal comparisons, 136-147
withdrawals from, 3-4, 7, 107, 114, 120-137, 132-133, 152, 154
see also higher education, withdrawals for; homebuyers,
first-time, withdrawals for; medical expenses,
withdrawals for

S

60-day rollover rule, 74-75, 111
S corporations, 21-22
safe harbor rules, 109-110
salaries, 9, 20
deferral of, see 401(k) plans
savings accounts, 18, 88
savings bonds, 10, 18
Schedule C, 9
Section 179 expenses, 22
Section 1031 exchanges, 22
self-employment, *see* sole proprietors
self-spreading of conversions, 87, 104-105
selling of real estate, 22
SEP (Simplified Employee Pension) IRAs, 6, 20-21, 74, 151
separate maintenance, and earned income, 9
short-term loan with IRA funds, 108
silver coins, 20
SIMPLE (Savings Incentive Match Plan for Employees) IRAs, 6, 20-
21, 26-28, 74, 151
single filers
and AGI limits, 10-11, 15, 32, 33, 34, 43, 85
and phase-out ranges of tax credits and deductions, 106
and Roth IRA contributions, 10-11, 14, 15, 34
and tax brackets, 49, 50
and traditional IRA deductions, 32-36
Social Security benefits, 9, 82, 102-103, 133-134, 135-136, 154
Social Security taxes, 25
sole proprietors, and expenses, 20-22, 26-28
spousal contributions, 12, 16, 32, 37-42, 44
spousal income, 32, 37-42, 44
state income taxes, 26, 54, 83, 92
state laws on creditors and IRAs, 113

stocks, 18, 19-20
strategies to reduce AGI, 18-23, 101
student loan interest deduction, 104-105, 106

T
tax brackets
    determining, 47-50, 70
    and IRA withdrawals, 3, 46-50, 53, 74, 76, 79, 81, 88
tax credits and deductions, and IRAs, 51, 106, 111-112
tax deferrals, *see* deferral of taxes
tax savings
    for sole proprietor parents, 26-28
    through tax-free growth, 45, 53
tax savings accounts, 54
taxable distributions, *see* Roth IRAs, and taxable distributions
taxable income, 48-50, 70
taxable portions of conversions, *see* conversions, taxable portions of
Taxpayer Relief Act of 1997, 1, 3, 7, 31-32, 86, 113
tips, and earned income, 9
traditional IRAs
    benefits of, 2-3, 47, 51
    deductible contributions to, 2, 31-44
    deductions for, and AGI limits, 10, 31-44, 84
    distributions from, *see* traditional IRAs, withdrawals from
    due dates for contributions to, 5
    due dates for establishing, 5
    and earned income, 32, 33, 37-42
    mandatory withdrawals from, 4, 132
    non-deductible contributions to, 2, 3, 31, 35, 73, 84, 127
    qualifying for, 2, 31-44
    and spousal contributions, 32, 37-42, 44
    withdrawals from, 3, 55, 72-74, 107, 110, 111, 114
transfers, trustee-to-trustee, 90
trustee-to-trustee rollovers, 75
trustee-to-trustee transfers, 90

U
unemployment compensation, 123

V
value of IRAs, 12, 54, 93

variables in choosing best type of IRA, 45-51, 154

W
W-2s, 9, 25
wages, and earned income, 9
withdrawals, mandatory, 4, 55, 132-133, 135
withdrawals from IRAs, *see* Roth IRAs, withdrawals from; tax
    brackets, and IRA withdrawals; traditional IRAs, withdrawals
      from
worksheets
    of annual income, 149
    of cash flow needs, 148
    to determine taxable income/tax bracket, 70

To contact publisher:

Conquest Publishing, Inc.
P.O. Box 543
Griffith, IN 46319

Email: conquestpublishing@yahoo.com
Or
Fax: 219-663-6484

Interested in future tax-related publications or newsletter?

Send us your email address or name and mailing address and we'll notify you when the next publication will be released.

Please indicate your areas of interest:

- **Individual tax planning/strategies**
- **Retirement planning**
- **Roth IRA changes**
- **Financial planning**
- **Small business tax planning/strategies**

Be sure to visit our web site:
www.rothira911.com